Amritam Gamaya

Lead Us to Immortality – Part 2

Amritam Gamaya

Lead Us to Immortality – Part 2

Śrī Mātā Amṛtānandamayī Dēvī

Compiled by Swāmī Brahmāmṛtānanda Puri
and Swāmī Vidyāmṛtānanda Puri
Translated by Rajani Menon

Mata Amritanandamayi Center, San Ramon
California, United States

Amritam Gamaya

Lead Us to Immortality – Part 2

Śrī Mātā Amṛtānandamayī Dēvī

Compiled by Swāmī Bramāmṛtānanda Puri
and Swāmī Vidyāmṛtānanda Puri
Translated by Rajani Menon

Published by:
Mata Amritanandamayi Center
P.O. Box 613
San Ramon, CA 94583-0613, USA

In USA:
www.amma.org

In Europe:
www.amma-europe.org

In India:
www.amritapuri.org
inform@amritapuri.org

Contents

Preface

Amma is a spiritual master showing the world the way. She is a mother helping her toddling children take their first steps. Through her actions and teachings, she has become a beacon for the world. Amma's precepts are backed by practice and personal experience; hence their undeniable authority. That is why her teachings always inspire her followers and awaken their hearts.

Having been born human, what is the foremost purpose of our life? How ought we to lead our lives? What are the things we must pay attention to daily? What practices ought we to follow every day? How are we to observe festive occasions? How are we to conduct ourselves with our colleagues? What ought to be our attitude to other beings in nature? What principles and practices do nature conservation and environmental cleanliness entail? Amma is trying to kindle in us greater awareness of these matters of utmost relevance.

'Amrita Ganga' is a compilation of Amma's messages on the above-mentioned topics as well as other contemporary and timeless issues. What you are holding is the second volume of this compilation. If we give Amma's priceless teachings the importance they deserve and strive to assimilate them, our life will become highly blessed; there is no doubt about that. We offer these precious pearls of Amma's wisdom to the world with the prayer that they help to elevate everyone spiritually.

Publisher

Awaken the Goodness

Children, we each create our own world around ourselves unknowingly. The fact is, depending on our nature, we take heaven or hell with us wherever we go.

Our thoughts and outlook influence not only us but those around us also. The goodness in some individuals expresses itself effortlessly when they are in the presence of certain people, who are able to boost their self-confidence and inspire them to do good. In their presence, those who are grieving become happy, the weak become strong, the wicked become noble, and the angry become peaceful.

In contrast, there are those who unknowingly abet the evil in those around them. Their presence fans the spark of negativity present in others. This is because they do not try to see the goodness in others, only their evil.

There is an ember of goodness in everyone. If stoked into a blazing fire, it will completely raze the forest of evil within. If we try hard enough, we can discern a speck of goodness in the worst sinner or the most wretched, and be able to uplift that person.

Repeatedly telling someone, "You're good for nothing!" will only inhibit the growth of his talents and rouse his evil tendencies. If we sincerely wish to awaken his innate goodness and help him grow, we must be prepared to acknowledge the good in him and praise him for it and help him overcome his negative tendencies and shortcomings lovingly and patiently.

Karṇa was a skilled warrior. During the Mahābhārata War, his charioteer, Śalya, repeatedly criticized and scorned him, saying things like, "You're useless! You don't have even the smallest fraction of the skills Arjuna possesses!" This stream of verbal abuse drained Karṇa of his self-confidence and strength.

Arjuna also had his defects and limitations. But Lord Kṛṣṇa corrected them all with love and patience. He constantly encouraged Arjuna: "Be mighty! Fight for the sake of dharma and defeat your enemies!" As a result, Arjuna emerged victorious in the battle. With timely encouragement and opportunities to correct one's mistakes, even a weakling can accomplish great things in life.

See Goodness

Children, only one who is able to see the good in others can experience peace and happiness in life. We perceive the world through the mirror of our mind. If our mind is tainted by suspicion, hatred and arrogance, then we will see only the flaws and failings in others. But if we look at the world through a mind filled with love, trust and humility, we will see goodness everywhere. What we see in others is a reflection of our own mind.

When we see the flaws and failings of others, it is our own mind that first becomes agitated. But when we can see the goodness in others, our mind becomes cheerful. Actually, being able to see goodness in everyone is of greater necessity to us than others. Not only that, when we perceive goodness in others, we will be able to deal with serious problems effortlessly.

There once lived a king who had only one good eye and one good leg. He summoned all the artists and instructed them to draw a beautiful portrait of himself. No one had the courage to paint the king. How to draw a picture of a man with only one good eye and leg and make that beautiful? As they stood confounded, one of the artists said that he was ready to do so. And he did. He painted a stunning portrait. Seeing it, the other painters were wonderstruck. The artist had painted a picture of the king hunting—aiming at the target with one eye closed and one leg tucked under him.

Like this painter, we should be able to turn a blind eye to the weaknesses of others and focus only on their positive aspects. Most of us notice only the negative aspects of others. Even if someone has a thousand noble qualities and one shortcoming, we will notice only the shortcoming. Like the fly living among dirt and excrement, our mind perceives only flaws and failings everywhere. We must transform our mind.

Nothing in this world is either wholly good or bad. There will be a sliver of goodness even in someone considered the vilest sinner. We ought to have an eye that sees goodness. If we try hard and with patience, we will be able to discern and rouse the goodness in others. Once we succeed in perceiving goodness in everyone and everything, God's grace will bless us abundantly. The foundation of success in any life is always divine grace.

See Goodness—2

Children, most people have a tendency to see the flaws and failings in others. Our minds are constantly agitated because we tend to do this wherever we go. We must change this outlook. Instead of seeing only the mistakes and shortcomings of others, we must try to see the goodness in everything. Doing so benefits us.

Dwelling on the flaws and failings of others taints our own minds. This habit robs us of the gains we have made through good thoughts. It is akin to acquiring sugar and then letting ants gobble it up.

Even if others make mistakes, we must try to forgive them. Forgiving is a penance of sorts, a prayer. God accepts the prayers of people who are forgiving. Conversely, no matter how much we pray, it will be of no use if we slander and hurt others. It would be like pouring milk into a dirty vessel.

During one Śivarātri, a child went to the temple with his father. Many devotees were staying awake and chanting the names of the Lord. A few among them were dozing off. Seeing this, the child told his father, "Dad, most of the people here are dozing off. What kind of devotion is this?"

His father turned to his son and said, "Son, it would have been better if you were also sleeping like them, instead of staying awake and finding fault with them."

We might ask how not to see the shortcomings around us. It is natural for our attention to be drawn to them. But if we try, we can escape from the clutches of this bad habit.

Very often, it is because of our own weakness or carelessness that we see the mistakes of others. Children, never forget this. Not only that, this tendency also reveals the extroverted nature of our minds. A mind that finds faults with others will not be able to recognize its own weaknesses and overcome them. Therefore, instead of finding fault with others, we should recognize our own flaws and failings and try to correct them.

There will always be some goodness in even the most insignificant object or person. But we must have the eyes to see it. When we become aware of the goodness in others, they too will become aware of ours. Thus, we can build a society based on love and happiness.

Cultivate Goodness

Children, all beings in nature, except man, live in accordance with their instincts. Humans have been endowed with the faculty of discernment, by which they can uplift themselves through effort. We have the ability to nourish our talents, cultivate good qualities and eradicate the negative ones. The goal of human life is also to achieve growth and expansion.

We must use every situation in life to foster good qualities such as love, compassion, patience, empathy, the readiness to serve others, and humility. Young children often test our patience by the way they behave. When their mother or father is engaged in some crucial task or entertaining important guests, the children might come and talk about some insignificant matter. Often in such situations, the parents will not have the patience to give their children attention or listen to what they have to say. They might scold their children or even spank them. They do not realize that they have missed an excellent opportunity to practice and increase their patience.

When love and patience fill the heart, life becomes a blessing. Conversely, when hatred and anger occupy the heart, life becomes a curse. If we are alert and strive sincerely, we can transform even adverse situations into stepping stones for our growth. To do that, we need an enthusiasm untainted by laziness.

Once, a man reached heaven as a result of his good deeds. God runs a special shop in heaven. There was a board in front of the shop: 'All goodness and wealth are available for free here.'

The man entered the shop. God Himself was waiting to welcome those who entered his shop. The man asked God, "Can you give peace and happiness to all the people on earth?" At once, God entrusted a sack full of seeds to the man. The man said, "This wasn't what I asked for, was it?"

God smiled and said, "Child, you will get everything from here but only in its seed form. You must strive to transform the seeds into fruits."

These God-given seeds of goodness are within each one of us. At present, they are still in seed form. If we water and fertilize these seeds and tend to them properly, they will grow into flowering trees of goodness and spread their sweet fragrance everywhere. Our life will become blessed.

Wealth & Peace

Children, money is one of the most important things in life. The misfortunes and difficulties that poverty creates in life are not small. Poverty stunts the very possibilities of life.

That said, anyone who thinks that having a lot of money will make life joyful is mistaken. There are many wealthy people whose minds are wracked by dissatisfaction, disappointment, fear, doubt and stress. Amma travels all over the world and has visited both rich and poor countries. Based on that experience, Amma can say that sorrow is no less in rich countries.

The US has only a quarter of India's population and yet there are 10 times more patients in mental health institutes there. If people in wealthy countries were free of tension and sorrow, why would there be so many people admitted to mental institutions?

Money can provide material comforts but it cannot buy happiness. Money might buy us many friends but it cannot purchase sincere love. Money can foot exorbitant medical bills but it cannot buy us good health. Money can buy us a house filled with all the creature comforts but it cannot buy a family life filled with love and mutual trust. You might be a multi-millionaire, but what does it matter if you are constantly living in fear that your children might kill you for your money?

There is nothing wrong with earning money; it is not contrary to spirituality either. The only thing is, we must understand that no matter how much money we have, unless we understand its place and practical purposes in life, money will give us only sorrow. This does not mean that we should live in poverty or that we must reject wealth. We must earn money through ethical means. Only then will our family life be secure. But let us not forget that if we make money through unrighteous ways, we will lose our peace of mind.

Having a mind that is content and happy with what we have is more invaluable than millions of dollars. Those who take only what they need and give the rest to the poor have understood the secret of happiness in life. Once we properly understand the place money has in life and its limitations, money will become our servant. We will become rich in joy and peace. If not, money will prove to be a cruel master.

Overcome Temptations

Children, if we sincerely wish to enjoy peace and freedom in life, we must learn to rise above difficult situations. One's true character is revealed in adverse situations. It is easy to fall prey to temptation and to become enslaved by the mind and sense organs but difficult to overcome them. Nevertheless, we must continue striving to do so. This does not mean that we should not enjoy the pleasures of life. We can enjoy them, but we mustn't allow our enjoyment to become an addiction. True strength is being able to live amidst sensory pleasures but remaining detached from them.

An alcoholic decided to stop drinking from the next day onwards. He made this decision with the bottle of alcohol placed right next to his pillow. His first thought on waking up was, "Should I drink or not?" While thus contemplating, his hand involuntarily moved towards the bottle.

It is difficult to overcome any addiction when temptation is near us. This is the principle behind the story of Vāli's death in the *Rāmāyaṇa*. Vāli had been blessed with the boon of receiving half the strength of anyone who fought directly with him. This is why Lord Rāma killed Vāli by firing an arrow from a concealed position. Vāli represents desire, which can never be overcome by direct opposition. To become free of desire, we must first distance ourselves from the object of desire and then strive to bring the mind under control. For example, if we wish to learn how to drive, we will begin learning on an open ground, away from the roads. Once we have mastered driving, we can drive confidently even on a busy highway.

Before we sow seeds, we will first clear the land of grass, weeds and mud clots, and then plough the land. We will continue to remove the weeds even after the seeds have sprouted. If not, the weeds will stunt the growth of the saplings. But once the saplings have grown into hardy trees, there will be no need to weed the ground around them because the weeds will not be able to harm the trees.

Similarly, if we are striving to gain control over our minds, we must, as far as possible, stay away from circumstances that are not conducive for gaining mental strength. But when we have gained control over the mind through incessant striving, we will be able to overcome any obstacle or temptation in the external world.

Ātma-kṛpa

Children, God is always showering his grace upon us. But to avail ourselves of it and let it benefit us, we need *ātma-kṛpa*, our own grace. There is no use closing the doors and windows to our room during the day and then lamenting over the lack of sunlight. Sunlight pervades the entire universe. To receive it, we just need to open our windows. Similarly, divine grace is ever flowing our way. To receive it, we must first open the closed doors of our heart. Hence, more than God's grace, we must first gain the grace of our own mind.

In India, students are given 'grace marks' to help them pass their examinations. However, to become eligible for those marks, the students must have a minimum score. One who has not studied at all will not receive any grace mark. Similarly, we need to put in some effort.

God is not just a judge who rewards good deeds and punishes evil ones. Above all, He is a treasure trove of compassion who forgives us for our mistakes and showers His grace upon us. However, he can save us only if we strive at least a little to become worthy of that grace. If we do not put in any effort, God's ever-flowing grace will not reach us. That is not His fault, but ours. He is an epitome of mercy.

To avert the Mahābhārata War and the annihilation of the Kauravas, Lord Kṛṣṇa requested Duryōdhana to give the Pāṇḍavas at least a house. But because of his egoism and antagonism towards the Pāṇḍavas, Duryōdhana repudiated that request. The result was total destruction. Duryōdhana lacked the ātma-kṛpa needed to receive the Lord's grace.

Newspapers regularly carry job advertisements. The advertisements will specify the educational qualifications, references and other prerequisites that the candidates ought to have. Even so, there will be candidates who meet all the requirements and who answer all the questions correctly during the job interview and yet do not get the job. The ones who get the job might not have answered all the questions correctly. The reason for this is that something about those candidates touched the employer's heart. That something is divine grace.

What makes us befitting of God's grace are good deeds. Therefore, even to gain the grace of God, we first need ātma-kṛpa.

Detachment

Children, God has given everyone the ability to stand apart and witness the experiences of life, but we are not always able to do so. When it comes to the problems of others, we can easily remain impartial, but we are usually not so detached when it comes to our own.

Suppose we hear the news of many people dying in a plane crash. We might feel sad for a while, but in no time at all, we will forget it. But if the fatalities had included family members, close friends or relatives, we are likely to have a mental breakdown.

A man attending a business meeting entrusted his personal mobile phone to his driver, who was waiting outside. After some time, that phone rang and the driver answered. A woman's voice said, "I just went shopping. At the jewelry store, I saw a stunning necklace that I absolutely love! I've never seen something so splendid before! Though it's really expensive, I just couldn't leave without buying it. As I didn't have enough money with me, I used your credit card to buy it."

The driver said, "Oh, that's great!"

The woman said, "One more thing. On the way back, I dropped by the Mercedes Benz showroom and really liked one of the latest models. As I don't have enough money, I sold some of our company shares online."

"That's alright!"

The overjoyed woman said, "I'm so lucky to have such a loving husband!" and hung up.

When the meeting ended, the businessman came outside and asked if anyone from home had called. The driver recounted the phone call. The businessman fainted. The driver was able to listen detachedly to how the credit card had been used and how the company shares had been sold, but it was more than the businessman could bear.

If we train the mind properly, we will be able to witness every circumstance in life and regard it impartially. Then we will be able to face the problems in our life with the same detachment with which we regard the problems of others.

Time Is Precious

Children, life and death are two sides of the same coin. Death is with us every moment. No one can say for sure that he or she will live to take the next breath. For this very reason, each and every moment in life is precious.

The only thing we have is the present moment. It is foolish to put off what we need to do today and daydream instead. The question, "What will happen tomorrow?" can never be answered. Calculating what might happen tomorrow is like adding four and four to get nine; four plus four will never become nine. Therefore, instead of worrying about the future, we should use the present moment in the best way possible.

A disciple asked his Guru, "O Master, please give me some advice." It was getting dark. As soon as he heard the question, the Guru began writing earnestly in the light of a candle. The disciple asked again, "O Master, please give me some advice." The Guru showed no sign of hearing the question and continued writing. The disciple kept asking his Guru, who ignored him and continued writing. Finally, the Guru stopped writing. At the same moment, the candle also burnt out.

The disciple asked, "Why is it that despite my asking you so many times, you did not answer?"

The Guru said, "I already answered your question."

The disciple said, "But I didn't hear any answer from you!"

The Guru said, "My actions were the answer to your question. I knew that the flame of the candle could go out at any moment. The candle could either melt completely or the wind could extinguish its flame. So, I did not waste even a single moment and focused completely on my work. Similarly, the light of life can go out at any moment. Hence, we must use every moment of life carefully. That was my message."

The only thing that is available to us always is this moment. It is like money in hand, which we can use as we like. If we spend it carelessly, the money will not benefit us much. We might be able to recover lost money but we can never regain lost time. Therefore, we must strive to use every moment wisely and thus proceed on the journey of life.

Empathy

Children, this is the age of machines. There are machines to do everything for us. Hence, some of us think that we don't need anyone else to become happy. Because of this thinking, we have become indifferent to whether or not others are happy.

Thanks to the advancements in science, we are now reaching out to distant planets. But the gulf between us and our neighbors is becoming ever wider. Even people living under one roof behave like isolated islands. Aged parents are being neglected, and children are being deprived of loving discipline.

It was different in the old days. Amma remembers her own childhood. Parents would feed their own children only after ensuring that the neighboring children had eaten. Parents would not be overly concerned if their children, who had gone to play next door, did not return home at night; they knew their children were in safe hands. Concern, sharing, and empathy for the pains and sufferings of others were spontaneous then. Those are the hallmarks of a true civilization. Today, our knowledge and information have increased, but we have lost our heart and wisdom.

Amma remembers the story of an expedition that encountered a tribal family living deep inside an African jungle. The poverty as well as the emaciated and dehydrated bodies of the people living in the hut deeply moved the expedition members, who handed over their food to the family. Instead of eating at once, the family members first divided the food into big and small portions. The explorers thought that the portions had been so divided with the elderly and younger family members in mind. They were wrong.

The father issued some instructions to the eldest son. As soon as he heard it, he took all but one of the portions and ran out of the hut. The explorers were puzzled. The head of the family explained, "He has gone to distribute the food to the other families in this settlement. The bigger portions are for families with more people, and the smaller portions, for those with fewer members."

Hearing this, a member of the expedition said, "But the food was meant only for you and your family!"

The father replied, "You shared your food with us. Shouldn't we also share what we have with others? If they are starving, our hunger can never be appeased. Their hunger is also ours, because they are not separate from us."

The mutual care and consideration shown by people we consider primitive is an eye-opener. The modern world needs to learn the first lessons of life from them.

Sēvā and Sādhana

Children, the Vedic scriptures say that it is only through *jñāna* (knowledge) and not *karma* (action) that one can attain ultimate liberation from the sorrows of the world. That being the case, what is the relevance of *sēvā* (selfless service)? Someone asked Amma this question recently.

The *Ātmā* (Self) resides not only in us but in all beings, moving and unmoving. We can attain Self-realization only when we see everything as one. We cannot gain entrance into God's world without the approval of even an ant. To become worthy of attaining God, first of all, we need to remember Him constantly and have compassion towards all beings. Once we gain this expansiveness of mind, spiritual liberation will soon follow.

We might go to the temple, pray and reverentially circumambulate the shrine three times. But if upon leaving the temple, we kick the beggar standing by the temple's entrance, we do wrong. Only when we can behold divinity in the beggar in the same way as we did the divinity inside the temple, do we become worthy of realizing God. We must serve all, seeing them as God. Only then will humility dawn in us. But we must take care not to think, "I'm serving the world!" Nothing we do with such an attitude can be considered sēvā. Real service is smiling, speaking or working with the attitude, "I am nothing."

Amma cannot accept it when people perform *sādhana* (spiritual practices) somewhere and then claim, "I've attained perfection!" Sādhana also includes service to the world. Only then can we find out how fruitful our meditation has been. A fox sitting by itself in a forest might think, "I've become strong. I won't shriek any more if I see a dog." But the moment it sees a dog's tail, it will forget everything and start shrieking. We should be able to maintain our composure while interacting with people, even when they get angry with us. Only then can we truly evaluate our inner growth.

We ought to see sēvā as sādhana, as an offering to God. If we can do that, then if someone expresses anger at us and even if our mind becomes slightly perturbed as a result, we will be able to reflect on what happened and regain our composure. We must think, "I say that I'm not the body, mind or intellect but the Self, and yet I became angry with him!" If we do this often enough, we will not get angry with anyone.

Performing austerities in solitude doesn't make one heroic. A truly heroic person is one who does not falter at all in unfavourable circumstances but forges ahead with single-minded focus. He alone deserves to be called a *tapasvi*, a man of austerities. Nothing can disturb his equanimity. Therefore, sēvā is certainly a part of sādhana.

Business Mentality

Children, the business mentality has seeped into every sphere of human life today and sunk deep roots in family and interpersonal relationships. No matter whom we see, our first thought is of what we can gain from them. If there is nothing to gain, we don't bother to form any relationship with them. If what we gained is lost, the relationship breaks. Today, even praying to God, making offerings at temples, and donating in charity have become like commercial transactions. That's how selfish the human mind has become. Society is now experiencing the consequences of that selfishness.

This attitude is like an infectious disease. When we look upon someone with a business mentality, unknowingly, that same attitude is roused in that person also. Gradually, this attitude contaminates the rest of society.

Once, an antique dealer was walking down a road when he noticed a cat drinking milk at the doorstep of a house. Though the milk bowl was dirty, he could tell from a glance that it was a priceless antique. He decided to trick the owner into parting with it. He approached the man and offered a hundred rupees for the cat. The man said, "Hundred rupees? Never! This cat is dear to me."

Scooping the emaciated cat into his arms, the antique dealer said, "Alright. Since the cat is so precious to you, I shall pay you a thousand rupees for it. What do you say? I'm sick and tired of rats infesting my home."

The owner reluctantly accepted the money. The antique dealer then said, "Friend, I paid a thousand rupees for this cat. Why don't you give me that old milk bowl as well? Then I won't have to go around looking for another one."

The man smiled and said, "No, my friend. This is my lucky bowl. Because of it, I've been able to sell 68 stray cats this week!"

We need business to live, but our life shouldn't turn into a business. Cultivating a mind that longs to love and serve others selflessly will benefit others and us. They will become well-disposed towards us. Even if we don't get anything in return, we will feel a lingering sense of pure joy. It is this attitude that paves the way to satisfying friendships and relationships. Gradually, both our life and that of others will become filled with peace and joy.

Friend and Foe

Children, the scriptures say that the mind is both friend and foe. The mind is the cause of bondage and liberation, joy and sorrow. If the mind is under our control, it becomes our best friend. But if we are controlled by the mind, then it becomes our enemy.

The mind is always telling us to do this or that. It will somehow keep trying to get what it wants. Based on its desires, the mind will convince the intellect to make decisions and to plan for the future. We can compare the mind to a marriage broker, who will try his best to convince us that every marriage proposal he arranges is an ideal match. If we are not careful, we will buy into his schemes.

A marriage broker once took a young man to see a prospective bride. On their way back, the broker asked the young man, "So, did you like the girl?"

The young man said, "You must be crazy if you think that I'll be persuaded to marry that girl. Didn't you notice that she has very bad eyesight?"

"Isn't that great?" the marriage broker said. "After you marry her, she won't notice it when you come home late at night."

The young man continued, "Not only that, she stammers!"

"That's to your advantage. Because of her stammer, she's likely to be quieter than other wives."

The young man added, "She has trouble hearing!"

"Don't you see how beneficial that is? She won't be affected by any gossip."

The young man lost his patience and said, "To top it all, she's a hunchback!"

"Brother, I feel sorry for you. She has so many good qualities. In spite of that, you're rejecting her because of one minor shortcoming. How will you find a better match?"

The mind is like this marriage broker. It will keep trying to bring the body and intellect under its control, so that it can fulfill its desires. We can never underestimate the mind's influence. And yet, if we sincerely wish to, we can bring the powerful mind under our control through discernment and relentless practice. Discernment is the understanding that bliss comes from within. Practice is repeatedly trying with utmost patience.

Through constant, intelligent effort, we can make the mind our friend and servant. Then, life will be filled with peace and joy.

The Power of Thought

Children, thoughts have a wondrous power. They mold our personality. What we think today determines who we become tomorrow. Similarly, our thoughts have the power to influence others. Positive thoughts create a positive mindset in people around us whereas negative thoughts create a negative mindset. It is similar to the harmful effects of passive smoking—when someone sits near us and smokes.

The vibrations of positive thoughts fill places of worship, āśrams and other such sacred places. When we go to such places, our mind unknowingly becomes calm and peaceful. Spending more time in places with an abundance of positive thought vibrations have a benefic influence on our thoughts.

Once, a king and his minister were traveling in the royal chariot through the marketplace. When they passed a shop selling sandalwood, the king told his minister, "When I see the shopkeeper, I feel terribly angry. I wonder why."

After making inquiries about the shopkeeper, the minister informed the king, "His business has been doing very badly recently and he is upset about it. You wanted a new bed, didn't you? If you buy the sandalwood needed to make the bed from this merchant, it will be immensely helpful to him."

Although he was reluctant initially, the king finally consented. In accordance with the king's wishes, the sandalwood merchant arrived at the palace the very next day with the sandalwood. The king happened to see him again and told the minister, "I don't know why, but today I feel an inexplicable closeness towards the sandalwood seller."

The minister laughed and said, "When you saw him yesterday, his business was doing very badly. When he saw you, he thought, 'If the king dies, many logs of sandalwood will be needed for his cremation. I can make a handsome profit!' His selfish thoughts stirred negative thoughts in your mind as well. That's why you felt anger towards him. But today, his prayer was, 'May the king live long! Then I will continue getting many sales opportunities.' The positive thought vibrations emanating from him touched you. Hence, you feel affection for him."

Our positive thoughts come back to us as goodness and our negative thoughts return as misfortune. Sometimes, there will be a time lapse between thought and consequence. Therefore, we must constantly strive to foster noble thoughts.

Learn to Love

Children, true love is exceedingly hard to find in today's world. We long to be loved by some people, but they don't love us. Others long to love us, but we are not ready to accept their love. Perhaps we don't like them. Thus, we are neither able to give nor receive love.

Today, most people form relationships with others only after thinking about how they can benefit from others. We must put aside our likes and dislikes or considerations of profit and loss, and consciously strive to love selflessly. Then, love from others will naturally flow towards us.

There are so many terminally ill people, whom doctors have said will survive for only a few more months. Some of them have told Amma, "O Amma, I want to love everyone. I want to love everyone a lot! I have hurt many people. If I see them again, I will beg them for forgiveness. Many have wronged me also. I will forgive them all and love them too. I used to fight frequently with my husband. I want to forget all that and love him with all my heart!"

Having come face to face with death and reconciled themselves to it, they are able to love everyone. Having accepted the inevitability of death, they understand that 'love is the only true wealth.' They realize that there is nothing else to gain, that nothing of what they earned can be taken with them, and that no one can accompany them when they depart from the world. When they know for sure that they have only a few days of life left, what can they do? Fill their hearts with love. Love and forgive everyone. That's all.

We can all awaken this attitude. We need not wait for a terminal illness to do so. We must understand that love is the only thing of any value in this world. The body is like a rented house. We never know when we will have to vacate. When that time comes, we ought to be able to leave in joyful celebration instead of tearful lamentation. To do that, we must first realize that worldly life is fleeting, and train ourselves to love others and to receive love from them.

Controlling the Mind

Children, among the emotions that control the mind, anger is one of the most powerful. When we become angry, we lose all self-control and the ability to think clearly. We forget ourselves. We become completely unmindful of how we talk and act.

At present, our mind is like a toy in the hands of other people. They know what to say to make us angry. When they praise us, we become happy. When they criticize us, we become restless. Our state of mind hinges on the words of others. When we lose our temper and create havoc all around, it becomes a spectacle for people to watch and enjoy.

Amma is reminded of a story. A man went to his regular barber. While cutting his hair, the barber said, "I saw your mother-in-law yesterday. She said that you're hoarding black money."[1]

Hearing this, the man's face turned red in anger. "She said that? She's the thief! She has borrowed money from so many people, but has not repaid a single penny to any one of them. I had to repay all her loans!" Even after saying all this, his anger did not abate and he continued to vilify his mother-in-law. The barber continued cutting his hair.

The next time the man needed a haircut, he went to the same barber. The barber seated him in the chair, picked up the

1 *Money obtained illegally or which is not declared for tax purposes.*

scissors, and said, "Yesterday, I met your mother-in law. She said that you don't contribute even a penny for household expenses."

Hearing this, the man started screaming in anger. "What right does that Tāṭakā[2] have to say that? I'm the one paying for all her expenses! I'm the one who buys her clothes and gives her money for food!" As he continued his diatribe, the barber cut his hair.

The next time also, the man went to the same barber to get his hair cut. As soon as he sat in the chair, the barber started talking about the man's mother-in-law. This time, the man asked, "Why are you always talking about my mother-in-law? I don't want to hear a single word about her!"

The barber said, "Look here, I know that you get angry when I speak about her. When you become angry, the hair on your head stands up. Then, I can easily cut it!"

When we become angry, anger becomes our master and we become its slave. But if we have true knowledge and self-control, we can change the situation. Once we understand that anger is a weakness, we will try to control it.

Actually, every person and situation we encounter is a mirror reflecting our weaknesses. Just as we use a mirror to remove the dirt from our face, we must regard each situation as an opportunity to rise above our weaknesses.

Controlling the mind becomes much easier when we understand spirituality. If someone gets angry, we can think that his mental weakness caused the anger and forgive him. Or we can reflect thus: "Why should I react in anger? I should conquer the ego, which is what causes me so much pain." Such reflections will help us maintain our equanimity.

2 *A demoness in the Rāmāyaṇa.*

Controlling the Mind—2

Children, anyone who wants to succeed in life must learn to control his or her thoughts and emotions. How do bad thoughts and desires come to dominate us? Negative emotions do not appear all at once. First, a thought arises. Then, a stream of similar thoughts starts flowing. Gradually, these thoughts become a strong desire or emotion, which grips the mind. A woodcutter uses his axe to mark an incision. Thereafter, he strikes that place again and again. This is also how bad thoughts become deeply impressed in the mind.

If we can uproot the thought as soon as it sprouts, we can easily curb our emotions. To do so, we need to develop awareness. Awareness means wakeful intelligence. When a man suffering from high blood pressure sees fried snacks, his first thought might be, "What a tantalizing smell! The snacks will be delicious!" The next moment, he remembers his disease and thinks, "If I eat this now, my blood pressure will rise, and I may fall unconscious. A blood vessel in my brain might even rupture, causing my body to become paralyzed on one side." When he thinks like this, he is able to curb his craving.

Once a thought has become a desire or emotion, it is difficult to control it. But we can easily do so before that. A man went to see his best friend at his house. The friend was not there, but as his wife knew this man, she invited him inside. Suddenly, the man realized how attractive she was. He even felt that he might not be able to control his burning desire for her. At the same time, his inner voice of reason advised him, "This woman is your best friend's wife. If you misbehave with her, you would be cheating on your friend. Both your families might be destroyed as a result. Control your mind, no matter how difficult it might be!"

Once his awareness was activated, he gained the strength to control his mind. This is why Amma always tells you to cultivate awareness.

Desires and emotions arise from the *samskāra*[3] acquired in past lives. If we keep pouring pure water into salt water, we can reduce its salinity. Similarly, we can overcome a negative samskāra by cultivating a positive samskāra. Noble company and reflecting on spiritual ideals help us cultivate a positive samskāra.

3 *A personality trait conditioned over many lives or one life: a mental and behavioural pattern; a latency or tendency within the mind which will manifest itself if given the proper environment or stimulus. It can also refer to the values one has acquired over time.*

Desires

Children, no matter how many people or how much authority and wealth we have at our disposal, our mind will never be satisfied. It will keep saying, "That's not enough. I want more!"

Once, a beggar entered the king's garden. He waited until the king was all by himself and communing with nature, and then went to stand in front of him.

The king said "What do you want? Tell me openly. Please don't talk too much and disturb my solitude."

The beggar said, "I'm a beggar. Please fill my begging bowl with something."

The king immediately summoned the treasurer and said, "Fill this beggar's begging bowl with pearls and other gems."

What happened next was strange. No matter how many pearls, diamonds and other gems were poured into the begging bowl, it never became full. In the course of trying to fill the begging bowl, the treasury was emptied. Even then, the begging bowl could not be filled. Seeing this, the king told the beggar, "Please forgive me. I tried my best to honor my word but I have nothing more to give you. This is a strange begging bowl. I long to know its secret."

The beggar smiled and said "Your highness, do not worry. This is not an ordinary bowl. It was made from a human skull. It will never be satisfied with whatever you give, and will keep asking for more. It knows only the language of begging: 'That's not enough. I want more!' No matter what you try to fill it with, it will never become full. It's like the human mind, which is constantly begging."

So long as we have desires, our mind will not be at peace. The happiness we feel when each desire is fulfilled is temporary. The very next moment, a new desire will crop up in the mind and we will lose our happiness. Therefore, before we try to gain what the mind desires, we must reflect on whether we truly need it. If we can give up unnecessary desires, the mind will naturally become peaceful.

Live with an awareness of the goal of life. Lead a simple life. Take only what you need and donate the rest to charity. Let us try to cultivate such a noble outlook. If we can do so, we will always experience inner peace and contentment even when we have fewer outer objects at our disposal.

Renunciation

Children, the ideal of 'simple living and high thinking' was deep rooted in the collective consciousness of ancient society. Such was the outlook of people in those days that they took only what they needed and set the rest aside for the community. But times have changed. Overly large houses, luxury cars, and inordinate wealth have become the norm. When the desire for creature comforts took precedence over values, unrighteousness and corruption became rampant.

If we put a plate of chocolates and a plate of gold coins in front of a young child, the child will choose the chocolates. But adults, who know the value of gold, will not do so. Similarly, people of discernment, who know the fleeting nature of sensory pleasures, will take the path of renunciation to attain the bliss of the Self.

There was a Guru who had many disciples living with him in his āśram. When they became spiritually mature, the Guru would send them out to serve the world. Once, the Guru decided to send a disciple to serve the world. The disciple prostrated to the Guru and prayed for his blessing. The Guru said, "Son, may you always be able to live in a palace. May you always get delicious food to eat. May you get to sleep on a bed of roses."

The disciple was astonished to hear these words. He asked, "All these days, you advised us to live a life of renunciation. Why then did you bless me to live a life of luxury?"

The Guru smiled and said, "The import of my words was also the same: that you should advance on the path of renunciation. While serving the world, the accommodation you get might be sparse or spartan. But if you have the right attitude, you will be able to accept the lack of comforts with a heart full of happiness. Then, you will feel as if you are living in a palace. Also, you must eat only when you're hungry. Then, you will find any food you get delicious. You should go to bed only after working hard and when you're very exhausted. Then, no matter where you sleep, even if it is upon a bare rock, you will sleep soundly. That's what I meant when I blessed you to sleep on a bed of roses daily."

Having understood the hidden meaning of the Guru's words, the disciple forged ahead on the path of renunciation.

One can attain immortality only through renunciation. Renunciation does not just mean reducing our creature comforts. It also means selflessly helping others.

Right and Wrong

Children, the scriptures say that God is compassionate. Some people ask, "If that's the case, shouldn't He forgive our mistakes?" God has given us the faculty of intelligence to discriminate between right and wrong. But often, we do not heed the inner voice of discernment. Then, we must face the consequences of our indiscriminate and arrogant actions.

God will forgive wrongs committed unknowingly or unintentionally. But if we knowingly do wrong and exceed certain limits, he will not forgive us. A young child might call "Icha!" or "Imma."[4] His parents will know that he is calling them and might laugh good-naturedly. But if he continues to call them that way even after he grows older, they will not laugh but scold or punish him and thus try to correct him. God might punish us even for our small mistakes. He does so only out of immense compassion for us and to save us. Such a punishment is like a lamp in the darkness, showing us the right way.

A child used to jump over a barbed-wire fence to get to the adjoining field. Seeing this, his mother advised him, "Son, if you slip and fall, the barbed wire will inflict deep cuts on your body. So, don't go that way to the field. You should take only the proper path there."

4 Corruption of 'Accha' and 'Amma,' which means 'father' and 'mother' respectively in Malayāḷam.

"Nothing has happened to me so far," the child said and continued to jump over the fence. One day, while jumping over the fence, he slipped and fell on the barbed wire, which cut his leg. He ran crying to his mother, who lovingly caressed him and consoled him. She then applied medicine on his wound. She reminded him again not to jump over the fence. But after the wound healed, the child started jumping over the fence again. He slipped and fell again, injuring his body. Crying, he ran to his mother, who applied medicine on his wounds and spanked him twice, not out of anger but out of love, so that he will never repeat the same mistake again. Similarly, the punishment that God metes out is an expression of His compassion for us.

In certain situations, we might find it difficult to distinguish right from wrong. Then, we must approach the Guru or a wise person for advice. We must thus learn what the goal of life is and how to live, and move forward along the right path.

Concentration

Children, many people complain that they are not able to concentrate while meditating or praying. True, it's not easy to concentrate. To make the mind one-pointed, we need to practice constantly. That said, not being able to concentrate should not stop us from meditating and praying. Unwavering enthusiasm and a focus on the goal can definitely help us gain concentration.

Amma remembers a story. There was a lad who did not possess any skill. His father earned his living by climbing coconut trees and plucking coconuts. When he died, people started calling the son to do his father's job. But what could he do? He needed to learn how to climb a tree first. Not seeing any other way of making a living, he decided to learn how to climb coconut trees.

He knew that he had to be very careful. If he fell down, he would break his arms and legs, and then, earning a livelihood by climbing coconut trees would be out of the question. So, he started practicing with great care. He hugged the tree tightly and started climbing slowly, placing each foot carefully on the trunk. After climbing a short distance, he would come down. After many days of concerted effort, he mastered the art of climbing coconut trees. Through practice, he was able to climb up and down quickly.

A spiritual seeker ought to think like this. "God alone is true. The goal of life is to attain God-realization. That is the only road to eternity. But there are impediments on the way. If I'm not careful, I'll slip and fall. Then, I'll lose my life." We need to have this attitude in order to gain concentration.

In truth, the mind is already pure and focused. But until yesterday, it has been home to innumerable worldly emotions. Hence, we are not able to concentrate when we sit down to meditate. These emotions are like tenants. We gave them the space to set up house in our land, which hitherto had been a vast and open tract. When told to leave, the tenants not only refuse, they also fight with us. We must struggle hard to evict them. We need to file a case in court. Similarly, to evict the tenants occupying our mind, we must file a case in God's court. The case will prove to be a constant battle. We must fight until we gain victory. Our inability to concentrate was our own doing. But through unceasing effort, we can regain concentration.

Thinking about our parents, relatives, friends or tasty food is not at all difficult. If asked to think about them, they will at once appear clearly before our mind's eye. We are able to spend as much time as we like with them because we have forged a strong bond with them through long association. Hence, we don't need to teach or train the mind to think about them. The mind is already familiar with them.

We can create such a strong bond with God also. This is why we must do *japa* (repeated chanting of the mantra), meditate and listen to satsaṅgs. We must practice remembering God constantly. Then, the form of God and the mantra associated with Him will arise in the mind as spontaneously as thoughts of worldly objects. Everything we see and think will be filtered through the perception of the Divine. There will be no world for us other than that of God. This is true concentration.

Through alertness and unremitting effort, we can gain such concentration of the mind. Children, may you all be able to do so.

Activate Awareness

Children, at present we have knowledge but lack awareness. We have intelligence but lack discernment. What we need are thoughts, words and deeds rooted in true knowledge and clear awareness. Without such knowledge and awareness, we won't reach our intended goal.

A cart drawn by two horses moving in opposite directions will not get anywhere. But if both horses move in the same direction, we will easily reach our destination. Similarly, if our thoughts, words and deeds are aligned, we can easily progress in life.

So long as our awareness is dormant, we will not be able to capitalize on the opportunities that come our way. We will act without thinking and land in trouble.

A businessman bought a factory on the verge of closure because of losses. In order to turn a profit, he would have to retain only the sincere and skilled employees and lay off the indolent and insincere ones. He started observing each worker carefully. On the first day he visited the factory, he saw a worker leaning sleepily against a wall. There were some men working nearby. He decided to teach them all a lesson. He roused the sleeping employee and asked him, "What's your monthly salary?"

The man opened his eyes, stared in astonishment at the businessman, and said, "₹6,000."

The factory owner opened his wallet, counted out some notes, held it out to the man, and said, "Usually, employees who are laid off are given two months' salary. Here is four months' salary—₹24,000. I don't want to see you here again!" After the worker left, the factory owner asked the other workers, "Which department was he working in?"

One worker said, "Sir, he doesn't work here. He had brought lunch for someone and was waiting to get the lunch box back."

The businessman in the story was intelligent, but he failed to bring awareness into his actions, and thus became an object of ridicule.

In order to do anything with utmost awareness, five factors must come together. One, knowing how to do the task; two, being able to tell right from wrong and being able to anticipate the contingencies of an act; three, a calm mind; four, complete focus; and five, the ability to stand back and assess oneself and one's work impartially. When these five factors come together, we can do any action perfectly. Let us all strive to do so.

Mutual Trust

Children, mutual trust is the foundation of human relationships. Relationships between husbands and wives, between friends, and between business partners can be sustained only if there is mutual trust. An awareness of our own mistakes and shortcomings often makes us suspicious of others and makes us liable to find fault with them. As a result, we won't be able to enjoy their love. We will also lose our happiness and peace of mind.

Two children from neighboring houses were playing with each other. The boy had some money, and the girl had a few chocolates. The boy said, "If you give me your chocolates, I will give you my money." She agreed and gave him the chocolates. The boy kept aside the coins of higher value and gave her a coin with the lowest value. Not knowing this, the small girl slept soundly later. The boy thought, "She must have had expensive chocolates with her. She must have kept them aside and given me the cheap ones, just as I kept aside the coins of higher value." Because of his suspicions, he couldn't sleep.

Some men tell Amma, "I suspect that my wife is in a relationship with another man." Some women tell Amma, "Sometimes, I hear my husband speaking in hushed tones to someone. Because of that, I'm unable to sleep." They married for love, peace and happiness. But because there is no mutual trust, they cannot enjoy peace and instead suffer terribly. As long as we are possessed by the demon of suspicion, we will not understand how baseless our doubts are, no matter who advises us or however much. Many families break up because of this.

First of all, we must be prepared to love and trust our partner. If we show them love and trust, they will reciprocate 95% of the time. Suspicion breeds suspicion, and trust begets trust. Before blaming your partner, look within and correct your own mistakes.

Most of the time, talking about our suspicions openly is more beneficial than brooding over it. If necessary, don't hesitate to seek help from friends and experts.

Being patient and generous with each other can help to bring warmth back into relationships. Above all, we must assimilate spiritual knowledge and learn to find happiness within. If we do so, we will be able to find happiness in our relationship with others also.

Do Not Waste Opportunities

Children, human life is fleeting. Like the rainbow, which appears momentarily and disappears soon after, our life must also make us and others happy. We must do good deeds while our bodies and minds are healthy. We must take care never to miss any opportunity to help others. We ought to consider such opportunities as strokes of good luck. Helping others will spread light not only in the lives of others but our own too. If we miss an opportunity to help others, the loss is ours.

Once, a businessman gave the supervisor of his company an account number and said, "This is the number of a bank account that I opened to help an orphan. Every month, deposit one tenth of our total earnings into this account."

For the first two or three months, the supervisor did as he was instructed. But when he saw that his boss never asked about it, the supervisor stopped depositing money into the account. After many years, the business started to fail. At the same time, the supervisor became chronically ill and was unable to do any kind of work. The businessman decided to sell his business and retire. Before leaving, he told the supervisor, "All these years, you worked sincerely for me. Don't worry about not being able to work anymore. I've kept some money aside for you. I'd told you to deposit some money every month into an account for an orphan. Actually, that money was for you. It will be more than enough for the rest of your life."

The supervisor was shocked. There was hardly any money in the account! Every month, he had splurged the money that was to be deposited on himself. Thus, his unrighteous deeds rebounded on him.

Most of us lead lives like this supervisor. We carelessly ignore the opportunities that God places right before us and then regret it later. "O God, I wasted all the wonderful opportunities you gave me. Today, sorrow and distress are staring at me. What can I do now?" What is the point of lamenting over lost opportunities?

Therefore, we must start learning to live wisely while we are young and healthy. We must cultivate a mind that feels compassion for the suffering. God's grace will flow only into a merciful heart. Grace is what makes our life meaningful.

Idol Worship

Children, someone asked, "Instead of worshipping the idol, shouldn't we worship its sculptor?" When we see the national flag, do we remember the person who stitched it? No one thinks of the tailor. What comes to mind is the country. Similarly, when we see an idol, we are reminded not of its sculptor but of God, the creator of the universe.

To appreciate the principle behind idol worship, we must first understand some things. God has no particular name, form or abode. He is the indivisible *sat-cit-ānanda* (truth-consciousness-bliss) that transcends space and time. That Truth is without form or attribute.

It is difficult for an ordinary person to worship the all-pervading divine consciousness without the aid of an instrument. At present, our mind is attached to many external objects. Idol worship helps to make an outgoing mind introverted so that it can realize the indwelling divine consciousness.

To see a clear reflection of our face in a mirror, we must first wipe away the dirt and dust from the mirror. Similarly, to perceive God, we must first cleanse our mind of its accumulated impurities. Through idol worship, the mind becomes pure and focused. This is why the *ṛṣis* (seers) ordained idol worship and temples in Sanātana Dharma.

Some people say that idol worship is a low level of worship. This opinion is true only if we think that God is confined to a certain place and form. If we worship with the understanding that God is all-pervading and immanent, then idol worship helps us gain an expansive heart. Worshipping idols and then insulting others is a low form of worship; so is worshipping different deities to fulfill selfish desires.

Those who criticize idolatry say, "Worship only God! Do not worship the devil!" True, we ought to live with the sole goal of attaining God. The devil refers to our unrighteous desires for wealth and position and to our selfish attitudes, not to the forms of God. The critics of idolatry often worship symbols or forms that remind them of God, not realizing that it is also a form of idol worship.

Even though God is beyond name and form, we can worship Him through the form we love. Even in one family, different family members may worship different forms of God. The father's favorite deity might be Śiva, the mother's favorite deity might be Kṛṣṇa, and the son's favorite deity might be Dēvī. This principle is known as *iṣṭa-dēvatā*, the form of divinity we most like. We must understand the principle behind worshipping the iṣṭa-dēvatā. Bangles, earrings, necklaces and rings are all made of gold. Gold is the substratum of all these ornaments. Similarly, God is the substratum of everything. We must see unity in diversity. Whether Śiva, Viṣṇu or Muruga, we must be able to perceive the same divinity in any form. We must understand that all forms are different facets of the one Godhead. As people have different natures and mental constitutions, the ṛṣis accepted the worship of God in various forms.

Through idol worship, we must cultivate a mind that is expansive enough to love and revere all beings. When we worship an idol, imagining the all-pervading God dwelling in it, our mind becomes pure, and we become capable of beholding and worshipping him in everything. This is the goal of idol worship.

Many *mahātmās* (spiritually illumined souls) such as Śrī Rāmakṛṣṇa, Mīrā, Āṇḍāḷ and Kaṇṇappa Nāyanār attained spiritual perfection through idol worship. Children, may you all be able to realize the Truth.

Rituals and Devotion

Children, it is good to pray at temples, perform pūjās, and go on pilgrimages. Our aim in doing so ought to be centering our mind on God. If we cannot do so, then all those activities are pointless. Customs and observances were initiated to help us to maintain the remembrance of God. Later, they degenerated into mere rituals. When we visit temples or pilgrimage destinations, we must go there with an attitude of surrender and maintain the remembrance of God.

There once lived a poor laborer who used to go to a Kṛṣṇa temple every evening and take part in the *dīpārādhana.*[5] One day, he was so busy at work that he could not reach the temple in time for the dīpārādhana. By the time he reached the temple, the ceremony had ended and the priest had left the shrine. The laborer became sad. A deep sigh arose from the depths of his heart: "What a pity! I missed the dīpārādhana!"

The priest, who knew that this devotee never missed the dīpārādhana, was amazed by his devotion. He asked the laborer, "I perform the dīpārādhana to the Lord daily. I will give you the *puṇya* (spiritual merit) I gain from this worship. In exchange, will you give me the puṇya you have gained by sighing with such deep longing?" The laborer happily agreed to this exchange.

5 A ceremony in which the Divine is worshipped by waving a lighted camphor.

The same night, the laborer had a dream. In his dream, Lord Kṛṣṇa told him, "You did something foolish today! Why did you agree to give the priest the puṇya gained from your sigh of intense longing? Even if the priest performs pūjās for his whole life, the puṇya he gains cannot measure up to your sorrowful sigh. The longing that arises from the depths of a pure heart is much more valuable than external rituals and ceremonies."

Children, all our rituals are meant to awaken our devotion and, through it, to become one with God. But we often forget this and become caught up with the rituals themselves. In love, there is no feeling of duality. Everything is the Lord. It is only because there is water in the river that there are two banks. But the two banks are united beneath the river. Similarly, when the devotee's love for God becomes deep, he becomes one with His divine nature. Therefore, we ought to pray to God, "Please help me forget everything by giving me supreme devotion to You!" This devotion is the only lasting wealth in life and the source of eternal bliss. If we gain such devotion, our life will become fulfilled.

Interreligious Dialogue

Children, there are many dialogues taking place between various religions and their leaders today. But along with applying logic, we forget to share the sweetness of the heart. What is required are not mere meetings but meetings of hearts.

"My religion is the greatest!" says one.

"No, mine is!" says another.

Such heated arguments haven't ceased. Religion has become a competitive arena. Owing to their narrow outlook and jealousy, people have not assimilated the key principle and message of religion.

Religion and spirituality are the key by which human hearts can be opened and we can look upon everyone with eyes of compassion. Instead, the heart is being locked up with the same key, thus creating even more darkness.

Once, four people traveling to a religious conference were spending the night on an island. It was freezing. Although each traveler had, in his bag, small logs of firewood and a matchbox, each one thought that only he had those items.

The first person thought, "Judging from the locket around his neck, he seems to belong to another religion. Why should I build a fire for him?"

The second man thought, "He's from a hostile country, which is always at war with ours. I don't want him to bask in the warmth of the fire made with my matchbox and firewood!"

The third man looked at one among the others and thought, "I know him. He belongs to a faction that's always creating discord among the followers of our religion. I can't bear the thought of him warming himself by the fire made with my firewood and match box."

The fourth man thought, "Look at the color of his skin. I hate his kind! There's no way I'm going to make a fire for him!"

In the end, none of them made a fire with the firewood and matchboxes they had. As a result, all four of them froze to death. In truth, they did not die from the cold outside but from their frigid and petrified attitudes. We are all becoming like them. We quarrel with each other in the name of country, caste, religion, race and color.

Today, thousands are willing to die in the name of religion but no one is ready to live for it. Religion is life, a way of life. But we don't understand this. We forget that spiritual principles are to be assimilated and practiced in daily life.

If we truly understand the principles of religion, we will feel the pain and joy of others as our own. Compassion will awaken in our hearts. We will understand the sufferings and difficulties of others and respond compassionately.

Problems start when we say, "Only my religion is good. Yours is bad!" This is like saying, "My mother is good. Yours is a prostitute!" For each person, his or her mother is the greatest. So, we ought to understand that one's viewpoint is important for that person. Then, our discussions will become fruitful.

Turn Within

Children, many of us despair when we encounter problems in life. In truth, there is infinite power and wondrous abilities within each one of us. But more often than not, life passes us by without our knowing of these powers and abilities or doing anything to awaken them. We have heard of instances when some people demonstrated amazing abilities when faced with great danger. If we are ready to quieten the mind and look inward with self-confidence, we can find the strength to face any situation and thus achieve success.

Once, a world-renowned musician came to perform before a crowd of thousands. The program started. The musician took up his violin and started playing. But something seemed to be amiss. Nothing he played sounded right. He looked closely at the violin. To his shock, he realized that the violin was not his! He hurriedly went backstage to look for his own violin but could not find it anywhere. One of his adversaries had replaced his violin with another. For a moment, he was filled with despair. The very next moment, he gathered all his strength and firmly told himself, "Music does not lie in the instrument. I will prove today that music is in my soul. May God bless me!"

He returned to the stage, bowed to the same violin, and started playing. The audience sat enthralled by the melodious flow of majestic music that issued forth from his violin. His performance that day proved to be among the finest in his musical career.

This incident proves that there is infinite power within us. In every person, there is music that has lain dormant for a long time. Our potential is boundless. Through effort, each one of us can discover and manifest that potential.

Similarly, all of us have the ability to control and uplift ourselves. Even people who consider themselves highly impatient show patience in front of their bosses. Even the cruelest criminal has tender feelings of love for his own child. There is patience, love, courage and compassion within everyone. The only thing is, it does not shine equally in all. If we look within and strive with awareness, we can awaken all the noble qualities.

The outer world will throw challenges at us. It will try to discourage us and make us withdraw. Then, if we look inward with a meditative mind, we will find a power and a peace that far surpass everything.

Jealousy

Children, from the moment we are born, society is constantly judging us and comparing us with other people. Therefore, it is only natural for us to compare ourselves with others and to feel jealous of people who are more capable than we are. As long as there is jealousy within us, it is impossible to have peace of mind.

Once, a woman from the US flew to Kerala to see Amma and to spend some time in the āśram. She loved the peaceful āśram atmosphere. As soon as she reached the āśram, she came for Amma's darśan. After giving her darśan, Amma told the devotee to sit beside her. As she had never before received such an opportunity, the devotee forgot everything else and sat there blissfully for a long time. Afterwards, she told quite a few people how happy she was.

The next day, she came for darśan again with great expectations. Once again, Amma told her to sit beside her. The woman's eyes welled up with tears of joy. After a while, she saw her neighbor in America coming for Amma's darśan. When she reached near, Amma told her also to sit beside her. The first devotee had not expected to see her neighbor, with whom she was not on good terms. She could not bear her neighbor sitting next to Amma. She started thinking, "What makes *her* worthy of sitting next to Amma?" She completely lost all the bliss and peace she had been experiencing until then.

She had spent many months working overtime to save up enough money to travel to India. Staying in the āśram for some time had been a long-cherished dream. But when that dream finally became a reality, she was not able to enjoy it. Because of her jealousy, she found each moment that her neighbor spent with Amma intolerable. This incident teaches us that when our mind is gripped by envy and jealousy, it is we who suffer most from its harmful effects.

Jealousy not only destroys our peace of mind, it can also cause great disasters that affect the whole of society. It was Duryōdhana's jealousy of and rivalry with the Pāṇḍavas, feelings he harbored from childhood itself, that paved the way to the Mahābhārata War, which destroyed the entire Kuru clan. For this reason, parents and teachers must see to it that competition among children does not escalate into jealousy.

Friendship is the attitude of rejoicing in the success of others. When we regard someone as a friend and help him or her, similar feelings will sprout in that person's mind also. When we cultivate friendship, there will be no place for jealousy.

Spirituality and Materialism

Children, we need not regard spirituality and materialism as separate. It is the differences in our outlook that make us see the two as different. Spirituality is the science that teaches us how to gain peace and happiness amidst worldly life. Spirituality sweetens life in the same way that jaggery makes *pāyasam* (pudding) sweet.

Those who desire worldly pleasures should also be prepared to experience sorrow because joy and sorrow are part and parcel of life. When the pendulum of the clock swings to one side, it is gaining momentum to swing to the other side. Similarly, there is sorrow behind every joy. This does not mean that we must renounce worldly life altogether. Amma is saying only that we must live in the world with an understanding of spirituality. Then, we will not suffer and despair.

There is a difference between the attitude of one who is about to attend a job interview and one who has been hired. The former will be tense, wondering, "What questions will the interviewer ask me? Will I be able to answer them? Will I get the job?" But the one who has been hired will be rejoicing. Similar is a life lived with spiritual understanding. One is no longer anxious because one knows that the happiness one seeks is within.

While standing inside the courtyard of a temple, we will not be shocked when the firecrackers start bursting if we know beforehand that they will burst at any moment. Similarly, if we live with an understanding of the world and its objects, we will not despair in the face of defeat. Suppose we need a lot of money and plan to borrow money from a friend. He might lend us the money or he might not. He might give us more than expected, or he might even pretend not to recognize us. If we are prepared for any of these eventualities, we will not despair, no matter what happens, because we already anticipated it.

A bird perched on a dry twig is ever alert, poised to take off at any moment. It knows that the twig can break at any moment. Money, position and friendships are also like dry twigs that can snap at any moment. Therefore, we must lean only against the eternal for support. Then, we will be able to face every crisis in life with a smile.

We must do whatever is necessary to succeed in life. The only thing is, all our actions must be founded on spiritual principles. Then, we can gain worldly prosperity. Just as Kṛṣṇa's presence ensured success for Arjuna, we will succeed in every walk of life if we live with values and a dharmic consciousness.

Overcome Depression

Children, it is rare to find someone who hasn't been gripped by depression at some time or the other. It is natural to become depressed when we face difficulties and setbacks in life. But we must not allow ourselves to remain depressed for too long because depression saps our health, willpower and mental agility. Let us not forget the saying that when one door closes, nine others will open. To unburden the heart, we can always talk to trusted friends, family members or relatives. If necessary, we must seek medical advice.

There are a few things that people suffering from depression ought to know. They should never miss taking the medicines that the doctor has prescribed. Just as we wear slippers to protect our feet, we must take the prescribed medication at the correct time in order to maintain the mind's stability. As the minds of the mentally ill are chaotic, they don't get sufficient mental rest. People with such a mind will not find it easy to control it or make it relaxed. The only solution to this problem is to resort to medication that helps the mind rest and relax.

The best thing that people suffering from depression can do is to throw themselves wholly into work. When they are engaged in activity, they will not be able to withdraw into their own shell. More than that, concentrating on work energizes the mind and makes it one-pointed. If they can work with discipline for some time, their minds will regain their health and vitality. Taking part in their favorite recreational activity also helps the mind regain its enthusiasm. All these actions can help them reduce the quantity of the medication they are taking for depression. But if they withdraw from all activity, their depression will worsen.

Spiritual practices like meditation also help those suffering from depression. However, meditation should be practiced only in small doses. Those suffering from depression should not meditate for more than 10 or 15 minutes a day.

People who suffer from depression are likely to express more anger and suspicion than others. But we should understand that it is not their nature but the disease that is causing such behavior, and we should be more considerate towards them. The depressed patient might even think that he is healthy and that others are suffering from mental disorders. Therefore, those dealing with such patients might lose their patience after a while. We must deal with them in the same way that we would handle young children.

Let us pray for those who are suffering because of depression. May their relatives, loved ones, and colleagues gain the strength to behave loving and patiently towards them.

Awaken Your Abilities

Children, God has blessed all of us with many abilities. At the same time, we also have many negativities and weaknesses. To succeed, we must identify our weaknesses, overcome them, and nourish our talents. We must learn to think creatively all the time. If we continue despairing over our weaknesses, failure is certain.

We must think about how we can capitalize on our talents. But often, people dwell only on their shortcomings. There are many skills hidden within us that we have yet to identify. But instead of trying to discover and nourish them, many people wallow in self-pity, and hence, their talents remain unused and become rusty.

If we decide to do so, we can turn even our worst weakness into a strength. Amma remembers a story. A young man who had lost his left arm in a car accident wanted to learn wrestling. He went to a teacher, unsure if the teacher would accept a handicapped student. But the teacher accepted the young man as his student without any hesitation and started training him to wrestle. For more than three months, the teacher kept training him in one move. Wondering why, the young asked his teacher, "Sir, all my other classmates are practicing many different wrestling tactics. But I have learnt only one so far. When will you teach me the other tactics?"

The teacher said, "It's enough for you to learn just this one technique. You can win a match with that alone." The young man was not satisfied with this explanation, but because of his faith in the teacher, he continued practicing the one technique that the teacher taught him with more intense concentration.

After a few months, the teacher organized a wrestling competition for his students. The young man also participated and won the first two rounds easily, much to his disbelief. In the third round, his opponent was formidably strong. Though he struggled, the young man eventually emerged victorious. Thus, the one-armed young man became the champion of the wrestling tournament.

The young man asked his master, "I can't believe that I became the wrestling champion. How could a one-armed man like me defeat the rest of my able-bodied opponents?"

The master said, "You mastered a complex wrestling move. Once you lock your opponent with that move, the only way he can get out is to twist your left arm. But it was impossible for him, as you don't have a left arm." Thus, the young man's biggest handicap became his greatest asset.

If we apply ourselves intelligently, we can turn even weaknesses into strengths. Similarly, we have the capacity for spiritual awareness, which can help us overcome all our weaknesses and limitations. If we awaken this awareness, we will come to realize the perfection of our true nature.

Meditation and Samādhi

Children, meditation is the easiest and most scientific means of making the mind one-pointed. Perfect concentration is known as *samādhi.*

The mind is an unceasing flow of thoughts. Samādhi is the state in which all thoughts have subsided, where there are no desires, and the mind has become absolutely still. In samādhi, the mind merges into pure consciousness. In that state, only pure consciousness exists. This is an experience of supreme peace and bliss.

Once, Goddess Pārvatī told her consort, Lord Śiva, "After you set off to beg for alms all over the world, I am all alone. You may not feel the pain of separation, as you are always immersed in samādhi. But it's not so with me. I cannot bear to be separated from you. Therefore, please tell me about samādhi. Then, I can remain here without undergoing the searing pain of separation."

Lord Śiva asked the Goddess to sit in the lotus posture, close her eyes, and turn her mind inward. Dēvī became steeped in meditation.

"What do you see now?" asked Lord Śiva.

"I see your form in my mind's eye."

"Go past the form. What do you see now?"

"A divine effulgence."

"Go beyond that and look. What now?"

"I hear only the divine sound."

"Go past it. What do you experience now?"

There was no answer. Dēvī's very individuality had dissolved. She had attained perfect union with Lord Śiva. There was no one left to ask questions or listen to answers. Dēvī had attained eternal and indivisible union with Her Lord. She had reached that supreme state of love, which is beyond the reach of words, the mind and intelligence.

There are different kinds of samādhi. In deep meditation, the mind might dissolve for some time. Then, one will experience peace and bliss. But that state is not permanent, as thoughts will rise up again after a while. *Sahaja samādhi* is the state of experiencing samādhi constantly even while immersed in activities of the world.

There is only bliss in sahaja samādhi. There is neither joy nor sorrow; there is no 'I' or 'you.' It is the state in which the mind has become established in the Self forever. There is no change in the state of samādhi, which transcends time and space. That transcendental state remains unchanged under all circumstances, no matter what activity is done, and even in sleep, forever remaining as enlightened consciousness. Others see the people who experience sahaja samādhi as living in this world of duality, but they are established in that transcendental state. They are ever reveling in the Self, and are of the nature of the Self. In their presence, everyone experiences soothing bliss.

Outlook on Life

Children, life is a mix of joy and sorrow. It is our mind and outlook on life that determines how we label each experience, whether as joyful, sad or disappointing. We must try to receive each experience with this understanding.

A writer sitting in his room wrote in his diary: "Last year was filled with disasters. I had to undergo a critical operation. After my gall bladder was removed, I was bedridden for a long time, and thus lost many precious days. For 30 years, I worked in a publishing house. This year, as I turned 60, I had to retire from the job, which I loved so much. My dear father died this year. His passing plunged me into sorrow. Disasters continued to haunt me. My only son met with an accident that wrecked my car completely. He broke an arm and a leg, and was hospitalized for many months. I cannot even bear to recollect it! The year that passed presented me with nothing but misery and misfortune."

At this point, the writer's wife entered the room. She read what he had written in his diary. She left the room and returned with a piece of paper that she placed before her husband. On it, she had written, "I suffered years because of pain in my gall bladder. Last year, I underwent surgery to remove it. It was such a relief! I turned 60 last year. I retired from my job while I was still in good health. I can use my remaining years to write in a serene environment. My dear father passed away last year. He was 95. He passed away peacefully without suffering from any disease or troubling anyone. He was undoubtedly a blessed soul. Last year was also the year my son received a new lease on life. Even though the car was wrecked completely, God gave us back our son without any handicap. The previous year was indeed a beautiful year, one in which God showered His bountiful blessings on us."

The wife saw in everything a reason to rejoice and be grateful, whereas the husband saw only misery and disappointment.

There is a silver lining behind every dark cloud. That said, we need to have an eye that perceives the silver lining. If our outlook is correct, we will be content and grateful to life. We will also be receptive to every experience.

Prayer

Children, some people wonder: "Why do we still have sorrows even after we take refuge in God? Why doesn't He hear our fervent prayers and fulfill our desires?" Such people lose their faith when the sufferings in life increase.

It is not practical to expect all our desires to be fulfilled because happiness and sorrow, success and failure are the nature of life. The devotion and faith of those who rely on God to fulfill their desires might increase if their desires are fulfilled. But what if their desires are not fulfilled? They will lose even the little faith they had!

How is it possible to fulfill everyone's desire? A doctor desires to have many patients daily, and prays for this to happen. If he doesn't get patients, won't he lose his faith in God? At the same time, those who are ill, pray, "O God, please heal us of our diseases! We don't want to be sick anymore." A man bought a hearse. Every day, he would pray to get dead bodies. Those who are alive pray never to die. This world is full of such contradictions. It is impossible for the desires of everyone to be fulfilled equally. Nevertheless, we can live in peace and contentment in this world of contradictions if we understand spiritual principles and live accordingly.

A machine usually comes with a user manual. If we study it, we can use the machine properly. If not, the machine will break down fast. Similarly, scriptural texts and *mahātmās* (spiritually illumined souls) teach us how to live in the world. If we live accordingly, we will be able to overcome any crisis and forge ahead. Otherwise, we will have to face sorrow and disappointment.

Most people turn to God only to fulfill their desires. This is not love for God, but love for the objects of our desires. If we depend on God only to fulfill our desires, we can never become free of sorrow. If we want our sorrows to end, our desires must abate. We must cultivate true devotion and faith in God. Then, God will fulfill all our reasonable needs. Instead of loving the trivial artefacts in the palace, we ought to love the king himself. If we can influence the king, the treasury will be ours! "Give me a job! Give me a house! Give me a child!" This is not how we ought to pray to God. Instead, we must pray, "God, become my very own!" If we can attain God and His grace, all the worlds will submit to us. But our actions must be noble, and our surrender, total. Then, nothing will affect our inner peace and contentment. Happiness does not come from objects. It is within us. But we mustn't allow external events to destroy our inner happiness. This is all that we need to do. We must be able to accept both joy and sorrow as His *prasād*, or gift from God. For that, we must have an attitude of surrender to God.

Impart Values to Children

Children, the foundation of success in life is the good *samskāra* (values and culture) we acquire in childhood. Every parent ought to bequeath to their child this precious and imperishable wealth. Actually, the efforts to impart a noble samskāra must begin even before a child is born. The mother must take great care to avoid situations that create inner conflict during pregnancy. Otherwise, the fetus's mental and physical health will be adversely affected. This is why it is said that a pregnant woman must remain cheerful, do spiritual practices, listen to satsaṅgs, and read elevating literature. This will uplift not only the mother; its subtle vibrations will also influence the child in the womb, awakening a noble samskāra in the child.

From the time a child starts remembering what he has heard, he or she ought to be taught values through inspiring stories. When the child hears Purāṇic legends or morality tales, he or she will unknowingly assimilate noble values. In order to mold children, parents must be ideal role models themselves. Otherwise, how can they raise children well?

In the past, a family consisted not only of parents and their children, but also the children's grandparents and other relatives. Today, people get their own homes as early as possible and leave the parental homes. Thus, the children lose out on the fertile soil of enriching family bonds. They also miss out on the many stories their grandparents could have told them.

Entrusting grandparents with the responsibility of raising the children when the parents go to work is ideal. They will bring up their grandchildren with more love and affection than hired helpers. At the same time, the presence of grandchildren will bring the elderly grandparents a lot of happiness.

The individuality of a child is shaped by the samskāra he gains until the age of five. During these formative years, a child ought to live with his parents. Nowadays, with the proliferation of day care services, the child loses out on the pure love and selfless affection of parents. Parents must take pains to compensate for this loss after they return home from work. They must somehow find time to spend with their children, even if it means taking leave from work.

Both love and discipline are needed. Children who did not receive the necessary affection while growing up will have more of an animal mind than an expansive heart. Conversely, if a child is overindulged, he or she will grow up weak and ill-disciplined. If a child makes a mistake, do not punish him severely but explain why what he did was wrong. True love for children does not mean taking them to the cinema or places of recreation, but imparting knowledge and values to them, because it is only through these values and knowledge that they will gain the strength to stand firm and not fall apart in adverse situations.

It is the immaculate character of the individual that paves the way to a country's progress and prosperity. Only when parents raise their children with a noble samskāra can an upright citizenry and society come into being.

Raising Children

Children, those who wish to create a noble society must pay utmost attention to the raising of children. Children must be trained from a very young age, when their character and values are formed. The earlier, the better. Ideas are easily imprinted on tender minds. What is imprinted then will also remain indelible. We must bear one thing in mind: disciplining does not mean punishing, and it should never be so. Just as a bitter pill is sugarcoated with honey, the mansion of discipline must be erected on the foundation of love and affection.

Until the age of five, children must be raised with a lot of love. Parents who sing lullabies to their children or tell them stories at bedtime must select devotional hymns, stories of the Lord, and morality tales. This will help the children maintain the remembrance of God. The seeds of nobility can thus be sowed in their subconscious mind.

The foundation of life is created between the ages of five and 15. Only if children are well disciplined can they walk the right path. If we shower children with too much affection when they are supposed to be disciplined, they will go astray. Instead of studying, they will become lazy. Utmost emphasis should be given to studies when children are in their school-going years. Care must be taken to provide them with relevant books to read.

After 15, children must be raised with a lot of love. Otherwise, they will go astray. Many boys and girls have told Amma that they fell into bad company because they did not get enough love at home. They long for love at that age, but parents often chastise their children at this time. Forget about loving them, some parents don't even allow their children near them. Instead of scolding older children, parents ought to explain to them why what they did was wrong.

We must never scold or criticize others in front of children; otherwise, they will imitate this behavior. Similarly, we must never find fault with our children in front of others. Doing so will affect the children's minds adversely.

There are those who believe that school-going children need not do any other work. This is incorrect. Studies are not the only thing needed in life. Children must be trained to do household chores.

We must impart sound values to children while their minds are still malleable. Even if they take the wrong path when they grow up, the noble values lying dormant in their subconscious mind will lead them back to the right path later.

Impart Values

Children, there are more and more complaints these days about how the younger generation has gone astray and are growing up without values. We cannot deny that there is some truth to this. But children alone are not responsible for this. More than them, the grown-ups are responsible.

Until the age of five, children must be raised with utmost affection. Our elders used to say that from the ages of five until 15, a child should not be spared the rod. But this is not practicable today. Therefore, grown-ups must set an example and become role models for children. If love and values are imparted equally to children, they will assimilate both and move ahead on the right path. But today, we see that even grown-ups lack an awareness of the right values.

A boy started going to school, where his father was a teacher. His son studied in his father's class. On the first day, his father taught the students that they must show compassion to the suffering. That evening, when a poor man came to their home to beg for alms, the father shouted at him and chased him away. Seeing this, the son felt deeply hurt. The next day's lesson was, always speak the truth, never tell lies. The boy took the lesson to heart. The next morning, there was a call for his father, who said, "Son, please tell the caller that I'm not here; I've gone out." Even though the boy did as he was told, he was very upset. The third lesson he learned in school was to have patience in life.

When he reached home that evening, he witnessed a bitter quarrel between his parents.

The next day, the boy did not want to go to school. When his father insisted, he said, "Father, you taught us to show compassion to the poor, to speak only the truth, and to be patient. But I don't see any of that here. I don't want such schooling!"

Nowadays, parents are only concerned about their children securing a good job and earning a lot of money. These will not make anyone a good human being. What is more important are values and social awareness. It is not enough to fill the petrol tank in the car. To start the car, there needs to be a battery as well. The values we impart to children are the battery. Values are what must be imparted first to children. To do that, parents and other grown-ups must first become role models for children.

Is Suicide a Solution?

Children, if we look at the newspapers, we will see that many people commit suicide every day. What prompted many of them to take their own lives was not illness or a lack of money, but mental fragility alone.

Today, if there are four family members living under one roof, they behave as if they are living on four different planets. There is no rapport between them; their hearts are not united. That's how rampant selfishness has become. Given this situation, if hearts are not strong enough, the number of people becoming mentally ill and committing suicide will only increase.

Some people poison their own children before taking their own lives. They don't stop to think about whether or not they have any right to kill their children.

What are the consequences of suicide? Even if a woman whose husband committed suicide remarries, the children from her first marriage might not be loved by their stepfather. Likewise, a stepmother might not love her stepchildren as if they were her own. Before taking the ultimate step, people ought to consider impartially what the future of their children will be like. Anyone who contemplates the consequences of suicide will gain the strength to withdraw from the decision.

We often hear about farmers who, having taken loans at huge interest rates, commit suicide when their agricultural ventures fail and they are unable to pay off their loans. If they are more discerning and patient, they will be able to live through the crisis. Once, a woman told Amma, "My husband took a loan, farmed the land, and suffered a loss. We sold the house and the land to pay off our debts. We then moved into a rented house. My husband and I work as laborers, and we are managing somehow on our meagre earnings. We spend whatever money is left after paying the rent, on our children's education and for our living expenses." Children from such homes have studied hard and gone on to become doctors and engineers. Many such families have done well through sincere effort. We cannot say what the future holds for us by looking just at our present circumstances. We can overcome any crisis through faith and hard work.

Many people see suicide as the ultimate way out of sorrow and humiliation. But what guarantee is there that death will end everything? Committing suicide is like going from dim light to the densest darkness. At the time of suicide, the mind will be terribly agitated. Such a mind will follow the self even after death. Those who commit suicide are like people who, scared of falling into a shallow well, leap into a deep abyss instead.

Many people take the decision to kill themselves when they lose the inner strength to face difficulties. We need to have the unshakeable faith that, "Come what may, I will face it bravely. I am strong enough because I am not alone. God is with me! The power of the universe is with me!" Then, we will gain the strength to overcome any situation. Even if there is just one person in every home who can understand the hearts of others and love them, there won't be so many suicides. Family members must support and shelter each other.

Path of Knowledge

Children, the root cause of all problems is ignorance of our true nature. How can a king who does not know that he is king discharge his duties as a ruler properly? How can he enjoy royal pleasures? We are presently trapped in such a state of self-forgetfulness.

The scriptural texts say that we are whole and perfect, and that our true nature is that of infinite peace and bliss. But gripped by the delusion that we are the body, we frantically search for happiness and comfort outside. This delusion is the cause of all sorrow. For this reason, the sole remedy for all our problems is right knowledge. Ask, "Who am I truly? What is my true nature?" Inquiring into the Self and discovering our real essence is the path of knowledge.

Each second, thousands of cells in our body die and new ones are born. Similarly, our mind, thoughts, emotions and intellectual abilities are all constantly changing. Yet, the awareness of 'I' remains unchanged amidst all these changes. Therefore, in truth, we are not connected at all to the body, mind and intellect. We are eternally free and of the nature of bliss.

Once, the goddess of darkness abducted the prince from the land of light and imprisoned him in a dark cell. She stationed many guards there to make sure that the prince could not escape. Sunlight seeped in through a small crack in the wall of his prison cell and advised him, "Give your crown and royal garb to the guards. They are greedy for wealth and will set you free."

The prince bribed his prison guards with his ornaments, robes and crown. They unlocked the prison doors and set him free. The sun god then gave the prince a sword, with which he slayed the goddess of darkness. When he returned to the land of light, the king anointed the prince the next king.

In this story, the goddess of darkness is ignorance. The sun god is the Guru. The ornaments and robes are emblems of desire. The sword gifted by the sun god represents knowledge. The inner meaning of this story is that the disciple who heeds the Guru's advice and gives up his desires gains the light of knowledge, which dispels the darkness of ignorance.

In truth, the experience of the Self is not something to be gained. It is always with us. We are of the nature of Truth. But ignorance has hidden from us the experience of the Self, just as clouds cover our eyes but cannot conceal the sun.

A child fought with another over a toy. He cried and screamed. Finally, he cried himself to sleep. While he slept, the toy slipped out of his fingers and fell to the ground. The other child took it and went away. The first child continued sleeping peacefully. Only the 'I' exists in sleep. Therefore, there is peace and joy. When he wakes up, the notion of duality—the sense of 'I' and 'mine'—and consequently, desire and sorrow, arise. Therefore, even while interacting with the world, we must gain the awareness of non-duality. Then, no matter what happens in the world, our inner peace will never be affected.

Blessing and Curse

Children, fortune and misfortune take turns to visit us in life. When circumstances unexpectedly become favorable, we feel blessed. But even under such circumstances, poor judgment and carelessness can lead to failure, and we might even face criticism and humiliation. At other times, circumstances might be totally unfavorable and they might seem like a curse. But if we act prudently, we can overcome those challenges and succeed. What we consider failure or bad luck might not be so in reality. How we face the blessings and curses that come our way determines the course of our life.

Kuntī served Sage Durvāsa devoutly when he was a guest in her home. Pleased with her service, the sage blessed her with a mantra that would enable her to beget a son with any god she liked. But this led Kuntī to conceiving before marriage and secretly abandoning the new-born child. Some people might wonder why Kuntī had to undergo such a traumatic experience even after serving a *mahātmā* (spiritually illumined soul).

Kuntī was not fated to have children. In his compassion, the sage wanted her to have ideal children after marriage. That's why he gave her the mantra. But wanting to test the power of the mantra, Kuntī chanted it before marriage. If she truly had faith, she would not have done that. Why blame the sage for an accident caused by chanting the mantra at the wrong time and without discretion?

A doctor prescribed a dose of powerful antibiotics to a patient, clearly specifying that the medicine was to be taken only after food. If the patient takes the medicine before food and becomes critically ill as a result, the doctor cannot be blamed. Similarly, Kuntī's sorrow was of her own doing.

There is another aspect to this issue. Ultimately, only good can come from good. The sage's boon later proved to be instrumental in eradicating *adharma* (unrighteousness) and reinstating *dharma* (righteousness). If dharma is to be upheld, those who are adharmic must be defeated. But initially, adharma will flourish. When adharma becomes rampant, God incarnates to uproot it. In the *Mahābhārata*, Karṇa sided with the adharmic and arrogant Duryōdhana. Knowing that Karṇa was supporting him made Duryōdhana even more wicked and egotistical. This led to Lord Kṛṣṇa supporting the Pāṇḍavas, and thus dharma prevailed.

The story of how Urvaśī's curse of Arjuna became a blessing is well known. The story teaches us that even difficult circumstances can be turned to our advantage if we act wisely. Because Arjuna followed Lord Kṛṣṇa's advice and acted prudently, Urvaśī's curse proved to be a blessing in disguise during his forest exile. Conversely, Kuntī's poor judgement and impatience made even Durvāsa's blessing the cause of sorrow.

Fortune and misfortune, victory and defeat are an integral part of life. However, we must not gloat in victory or despair in failure. If we act intelligently and with unshakeable self-confidence and faith in God, we can overcome all obstacles and attain success in life.

Boredom

Children, there are few people who do not get bored. Boredom affects young children, the youth and the aged alike. We experience boredom not only when we are alone but also when we are with family and friends. Boredom strikes us not only when we are doing nothing, it also assails us when do the same task continuously.

The music that we hear when we call someone on the phone is meant to prevent us from getting bored while waiting for the caller to answer. Many people can't remain still even for such a short time. They become restless and fed up. That is why there is so much graffiti in the notebook, on the table and elsewhere in a public phone booth.

No object in the world, whatever it may be, can make us happy for long. The tastiest dish or the finest song or job will lose its novelty after a while, and then boredom will set in.

Amma is reminded of a story. A man felt strongly attracted to a Miss World and desperately wanted to marry her. He got an opportunity to meet and be introduced to her. Their friendship blossomed into love and they eventually got married. The man would constantly think of her, no matter what he was engaged in, and this gave him untold joy. But within a few months, the situation altered dramatically. He started finding fault with her character and conduct. Gradually, he started losing interest in her until he found even her presence intolerable. Finally, they divorced each other. This is what the world is like today. Whether Mr. or Miss Universe, once the novelty wears off, the exhilaration and joy we initially felt in his or her company will wane. Finally, we will get bored.

How can we overcome boredom? Instead of facing it, many people run away from it and seek solace in alcohol, drugs and overeating. These habits not only harm the health of body and mind. When the 'high' disappears, boredom sets in and grabs us with even greater force. Other people try to overcome boredom through recreational activities. Here, too, there is a problem: that tactic does not work all the time. For example, to deal with boredom, we might decide to go for a picnic or drive to the beach. On the way there, we might get caught in traffic. We will face boredom again. Thus, if we try to escape boredom, we will run straight into it.

We must first understand that the mind cannot find joy in any worldly object for long. The source of all joy is within us. We must train ourselves to find and awaken this inner joy without leaning against any external object. If we succeed in doing so, then we can remain enthusiastic and cheerful no matter what we are doing or even if we are not doing anything.

The medicine that cures boredom is neither money nor power but the ability to forget everything and dissolve the mind into oneself. He who has this skill, whether he be rich or poor, is the happiest man in the world.

The Illusory Universe

Children, many people ask why this world is considered 'Māyā' or illusory. Māyā is that which veils and distances us from the Truth. Māyā is that which cannot give us lasting peace. We run after the experiences and objects of the world, believing them to be true. Thus, we become estranged from the Truth and forgo everlasting peace. For the dreamer, the dream world is real. But when he wakes up, he realizes it was never real. Similarly, we are now in dream caused by Māyā. Only when we awaken from this dream will we know the Truth.

A poor, young man was sitting beside a river and fishing. After a while, he saw an elephant approaching. It was holding a garland with its trunk. A crowd of people was following the elephant. The elephant garlanded the young man, and a roaring cheer arose from the crowd.

This was the ritual by which the heir to the throne was selected. The man whom the elephant adorned with the garland, which had been offered to the deity in the main temple of the kingdom, would be anointed heir to the throne. Thus, the young man became the heir apparent and married the princess.

One day, the princess and the young man went horse riding on a mountain top near the palace. Suddenly, a gale knocked down the horse and the royal couple. The fall killed the horse and the princess. The prince grabbed a branch of a tree and saved himself. He carefully let go of the branch and looked around. He could not see the forest, the princess, the horse or the palace. He saw only the mud walls of his hut. Not having eaten anything for two days, he had returned to his hut and laid down. Exhausted, he fell asleep at once. When he woke up, he realized that all that he had experienced was only a dream. He did not feel upset that he had lost his kingdom and princess because he knew that the whole thing had only been a dream, even though it had all felt very real during the dream. At present, we are all like this young man. If we awaken from the dream of worldly life that we are seeing now, we will not be affected by its victories and failures, gains and losses.

If the world is illusory, how should we approach it? Should we deny it? Definitely not. If we approach the world and its objects intelligently, they will become guides leading us to the Truth. Then, we will be able to perceive goodness in everything. A murderer uses a knife to kill people whereas a doctor uses one to save countless lives. Therefore, instead of rejecting everything as illusory, understand the true nature of every object and make practical use of it in life.

Those who know Māyā save the world. They never fall under Māyā's spell. But those who do not understand Māyā will not only destroy themselves but also become a burden to others. One who sees only the good in everything can never see anything as Māyā. Everything leads him to goodness.

Grace and Surrender

Children, we strive for many things every day. Of these, we succeed in getting only a few. We might drive very carefully. Yet, if there is a careless or drunk driver coming from the opposite side, he might crash into us. Similarly, even if a student prepares thoroughly for an examination, she might not get the marks she deserves if the examiner grading the paper is careless. Why do such things happen? No matter how talented or hardworking we may be, our efforts will be crowned with success only if God's grace is with us.

One day, Bhīma[6] was walking alone in the forest. Suddenly, he spotted a pregnant doe in the distance. The deer started at the sight of Bhīma. She glanced in the four directions and stood petrified. When Bhīma looked all around, he understood why the deer was behaving this way. A lion was waiting in front to pounce on her; it was waiting because there was a hunter behind her, his arrow trained on her. To her right was a rapid river, and to her left, a forest fire was burning fiercely. The deer was surrounded on all four sides by dangers.

Seeing the doe's plight, Bhīma's heart melted, but he was helpless. If he tried to chase the hunter away, the frightened deer would run straight into the jaws of the lion. If he tried to put out the forest fire, the doe would leap into the river in a panic and be swept away by its swift currents. Seeing no way

6 *One of the five Pāṇḍava brothers; character in the Mahābhārata.*

to save her, Bhīma finally called out to God: "O Lord, I'm totally helpless. Only you can save the deer. Please save her!"

The very next moment, there was a loud clap of thunder. Heavy rains began pouring down. The hunter was struck by lightning and fell unconscious. The rain extinguished the forest fire. The lion ran away, frightened. As soon as the threats around her disappeared, the deer fled to safety. Seeing all this, Bhīma stood transfixed in astonishment.

When we understand the limits of our abilities and appreciate God's infinite glory, we will realize that only divine grace can make our efforts fruitful. Bhīma became befitting of God's grace because of his compassion for the deer and his surrender to the Divine. When effort, compassion and surrender come together, God will definitely shower His grace.

Become a Good Listener

Children, if we wish to succeed in any action, we must become good listeners.

We usually talk about what we know. But to gain more knowledge, we must be ready to listen carefully to what others say. God has given us two ears that are always open and a mouth that can be closed. This shows that listening is more important than talking.

When people talk to us, many of us are mentally preparing our answer to them. But a good listener pays total attention to what the other person is saying. Then, both speaker and listener become of one mind. As a result, real communication takes place.

Listening attentively is the hallmark of a generous mind. We might not be capable of helping the person speaking to us but it is enough for us to listen sympathetically. That itself will give the speaker much solace. What lends beauty to the ears are not earrings but the ability to listen with compassion to the problems of others.

Listening plays a big part in maintaining harmonious family relationships. These days, no one has either the time or the patience to listen attentively to what others say. Once, a woman told her friend, "I'm confident that any secret I tell my husband will not be divulged."

The friend asked, "Do you trust him so much?"

"Not that, but he never pays attention to anything I say."

When our loved ones talk to us, it is not enough to listen with our ears, we must also listen with our hearts.

Listening attentively is a great way of expressing our interest in and respect for the speaker. When we listen attentively to someone, we understand not just the words but also the real sentiments behind his or her words. One reason for most interpersonal conflicts is that no real communication takes place. Many problems can be solved if we listen attentively to what others say.

As the mind becomes increasingly silent, we will be able to hear the voice of our conscience ever more clearly. That voice is very soft but it is what leads us to goodness. Therefore, we must never ignore it. If we listen to that voice attentively, we will not go astray but be able to walk the straight path in life.

Desire and Pleasure

Children, some people ask, "Didn't God give us a body and create objects of pleasure so that we can enjoy those objects and live comfortably?" Amma isn't saying that we should not enjoy pleasures but that everything should be within limits. We must not abandon dharma. Living an unrestrained life leads to sorrow, not happiness. It is natural for the mind to harbor desires but we must exercise some control over them.

Just because there are good macadam roads and bright street lights does not mean that we can drive any way we like; if we do so, we might meet with an accident and die. While driving, we must obey traffic rules. Similarly, when we live in this world, which is God's creation, we must follow certain rules, or suffer the consequences. Chocolates are delicious, but if we gorge on them, we will get a stomach ache. Anything excessive becomes a cause of sorrow. Therefore, eat only as needed, talk only when necessary, and sleep only when necessary. Spend the rest of the time doing good deeds. Do not waste even a single moment of your life. See to it that your life becomes beneficial to others also.

The waves of the ocean rise up with a roar. The very next moment, they crash onto the shore. The waves cannot remain suspended above for more than a moment. Similarly, man, who eagerly leaps for objects in the mistaken belief that they will give him happiness, lands in sorrow. The mind that seeks pleasure outside can never find true happiness. The search always ends in disappointment.

We must understand that worldly objects cannot give us lasting happiness. If we cover a lighted lamp with a pot that has a hole in it, light will stream out through the hole. But the source of the light is not the hole. Similarly, the source of happiness is not external objects but the Self. A calm mind is naturally happy, but we ourselves often cover it up with desires and complaints.

Many people say that curbing desires is next to impossible. But once we understand the nature of worldly joy, we will find that it is not so difficult. Would we allow a man, whom we know will harm us, to stay with us? No, because we know that he might harm us at any moment. No one keeps a rabid dog or poisonous snake as a pet. We take pains to stay away from them. Similarly, if we live with an understanding of the true nature of sensory pleasures, we won't suffer but enjoy peace and happiness in life.

Peace Through Goodness

Children, it is the nature of the human mind to find fault wherever it goes. We don't realize that when we do so, it is our own mind that becomes unsettled. Overlook the shortcomings, focus on what we can gain, and respect that. If we can do this, we will find that our sufferings will lessen.

If there is goodness within, we will perceive goodness everywhere. At the sight of a lotus growing in a marsh, a mind filled with goodness will perceive and appreciate only the beauty of the flower. If the mind focuses on the marsh instead, it will become uneasy.

Once, a man visited the āśram of a *mahātmā* (spiritually illumined soul). After bowing down to the mahātmā, he said, "To this day, I have not knowingly hurt anyone. Since childhood, I have been taught that 'Kind words go a long way.' Therefore, I always speak carefully so that my words don't hurt anyone." He then gave an example to explain why harsh words are unpleasant. "On the days I stay here in the āśram, I hear the chirping of the birds at dawn and dusk. The cuckoo's song and the warbling of other birds are pleasant, but the cawing of the crows is harsh. When I hear it, I feel such loathing!" Having said that, the man revealed something that was making him sad: "Even though I have spoken only kind words, the journey of my life hasn't been smooth. Why?"

While the man was speaking, the mahātmā had been drawing a picture on the sand with her fingertip. Without looking up, the mahātmā smiled and said, "Try also to love the crow, which does not have a melodious voice. If you can bring yourself to like its cawing, your mind will fill with happiness. Not only that, you will become more befitting of God's grace." Saying so, the mahātmā became silent. Those words contained all the answers to the man's question.

When a sculptor sees a stone or a piece of wood, he immediately perceives the sculpture hidden within. But others will see it only as a stone or a piece of wood. We ought to be like the sculptor and perceive the good in everything.

Trying to see the goodness in others will do more good than chanting our mantra a million times. Such people need not go anywhere in search of anything. God will provide whatever they need. Happiness will become second nature to them.

Scriptures and Life

Children, the scriptures are the teachings of those who have realized the Truth. The scriptures help us distinguish between right and wrong and to walk the right path to attain the goal of life. Through scriptural study, the road to Self-realization will soon become clear to us.

We must try to understand the essence of the scriptures and assimilate it in life. Otherwise, scriptural study is of no use. If a man who wants to go to Kanyakumari merely stands and stares at the roadside signboard showing the way there, how is that going to help him?

Gain peace and contentment in life; learn to love and respect everyone; and maintain composure in adverse circumstances—these are what we ought to attain through scriptural study. Any scriptural study that does not help us gain these qualities is a waste. We must overcome the tendency to misinterpret scriptural statements and spiritual principles to rationalize our flaws and failings.

Once, a traveler was sitting under a tree right in front of a Dēvī temple and smoking. Seeing this, the priest sternly told him, "Look, this is a sacred place. Please do not sit here and smoke."

The traveler retorted angrily, "I'm no one's slave! I am my own boss! I don't like anyone trying to control me. I know what to do and what not to do. The flame in the lamp in front of the Dēvī idol and the fire that lit my cigarette are one and the same. I see Dēvī in both. That being the case, what's wrong with smoking?"

Hearing this, the priest said, "If you can perceive Dēvī in everything, then you would not try to find happiness in the cigarette. You are addicted to smoking. You've still not understood the scriptural truth that one can never find true happiness in external objects. The source of true happiness is within us. Not only that, one who beholds God in everything will never behave this way. Such a person will always be a role model to others. Their every word and deed will inspire others to walk the path of goodness. You have perverted a spiritual principle to mask your own mistakes and shortcomings. We must first recognize our own weaknesses, accept them and then overcome them. Only then can we say, 'I am my own boss.'"

Children, may you interpret the scriptures intelligently and thus be able to make your life blessed.

Problems and Opportunities

Children, there is only one thing we have too much of in this world: problems. Any situation that we find difficult to handle is a problem for us.

There are different kinds of problems. Some are based on clear facts such as a lack of food, clothing, shelter and health. But there are also problems that have their roots in our imagination: anxiety about the future, worry about whether personal relationships will last, or fear about whether or not the plane we are in will crash, among others.

There are two kinds of people in the world: those who see every situation in life as a problem, and those who regard every situation in life as an opportunity. Most people are of the first kind. Like the demon Bhasmāsura, who reduced everything he touched into ash, they turn anything and everything into a problem.

A young man wanted to marry a farmer's daughter. When he asked the farmer for permission, the farmer said, "I shall give you a test. If you pass the test, you can marry my daughter. I shall release three bulls, one after another, from the bull pen. If you can cling to the tail of any one of the bulls, you will pass the test."

The young man waited for the bulls to come out. The farmer opened the pen and released a huge bull. The young man was stunned. He felt it would be foolish to try and grab its tail. There were two bulls left. He decided to try and grab the tail of one of them. After a while, the pen was opened again. The bull that came out was so massive that the first bull paled in comparison. The young man did not even dare to go near the animal. He waited for the third bull to emerge. This time, when the pen was opened, a smile lit up his face. The bull that came out was the smallest he had ever seen! When he ran to grab its tail, he realized that it had no tail!

When opportunities come our way, we usually do not recognize them because they often come in the guise of problems and challenges. If we can see them as opportunities for us to identify our weaknesses, rise above them, and thus gain the strength to overcome them, we will succeed. That is why we must first change our mindset.

Gratitude

Children, nowadays everyone knows only how to take from others. Not many people have a heart that wants to give and help others. Everyone is acquainted with his or her rights but doesn't show much interest in fulfilling responsibilities. We are indebted to our parents, friends, colleagues and, above all, nature. Instead of considering all that we have taken and gained from them as an entitlement, we must be prepared to discharge our duty to them with gratitude.

A beggar went to beg for alms at a house. He had been going there for many years. That day, the man of the house gave him ₹10. The beggar became angry and told the man, "In the early years, you used to give me ₹100 every month. Then you reduced it to ₹50. After a few more years, it became ₹25. Now, you have given me only ₹10. Is this reasonable?"

The man said, "When you first started coming, I was unmarried and so could spare ₹100. Then I got married. My wife isn't working. My expenses increased. That's why I reduced the alms to ₹50. Later, I had a child. The expenses increased even further. So, I reduced the alms to ₹25. We've just had another baby. To tell you the truth, I don't have money to give you. But I felt that I should give you something at least. That's why I'm giving you ₹10."

When he heard this, the beggar shouted angrily, "How dare you maintain your family with my money!"

Many of us often behave like this beggar, who felt entitled to the money instead of receiving the alms with gratitude. We behave selfishly towards nature, our fellow beings, family and friends. Instead of expressing gratitude for the help we receive from others, we act as if we are entitled to it. The ethos of being thankful to others is fading from society.

We are always expecting something from others. Let us not forget that they are also expecting many things from us. We must try to understand what those expectations are and strive to fulfill them. If we can develop a mind that longs to give rather than take, we will gain peace of mind.

The Goal of Spiritual Practice

Children, many people seem to have wrong notions about what spiritual practices are and what their aims are. Remaining strong in difficulties, seeing God in everyone, and loving everyone equally—this is what we should gain through *sādhana* (spiritual practice). The highest goal of all sādhana is the ability to maintain an unshakeable inner peace amidst the ups and downs of life.

The purpose of meditation, *japa* (repeated chanting of a mantra) and other practices is not to gain some paranormal experience. Some people say that they see a green or red light during meditation. Once, a man told Amma, "I always see a green light when I meditate."

Amma said, "In that case, please don't drive any vehicle, son, because you will see the red traffic light as green and will not stop your car." It is not to gain such experiences that we practice meditation and other forms of sādhana. The real aim of sādhana is to gain equanimity and peace of mind.

Some people inhale and exhale forcefully. When this is done continuously, the *prāṇa* (vital breath) in our head will decrease, and we will feel as if we are soaring into another world. This is not spiritual bliss. When their vision becomes dim, some spiritual seekers tell Amma that they see lights in their eyes. They don't realize that it is because there is a problem in their eyes. Instead, these people explain it as if they were seeing the effulgence of the Self. Amma advises them to see an ophthalmologist. Once the disease is treated, they will stop seeing the light.

Even if we get certain experiences as a result of our spiritual practice, we need not take them too seriously. They are also like dreams. If a beggar dreams that he has become a king, will that help him in real life? What we need is an inner poise in each and every situation while we are awake. That is real spiritual progress. Through spiritual practice, we must regain the natural peace and calm of the mind. We must develop the ability to remain patient under any circumstance. We must learn to see goodness in everything. This is true spiritual progress.

Self-realization is being able to see oneself in all beings, and thus love and serve them. This is the culmination of sādhana.

New Year

1

Children, the dawn[7] of a New Year is an auspicious occasion to make a fresh start and an opportune moment to release sorrowful memories. We must be ready to learn from the past and, in the light of our new understanding, make changes to our life and lifestyle.

Life is like a garden. It is natural for leaves to wither and for flowers to wilt. Only if we clear away this debris regularly can we enjoy the beauty of new sprouts and blossoms in the garden. So, let us brush away the turmoil of the past, forgive what ought to be forgiven, forget what ought to be forgotten, and embrace life with renewed zest.

Life should not turn into a sprint for success. There are many people around us who are less fortunate. We ought to spend some time with them and try to understand their pains, sorrows and difficulties.

Today, everyone aspires to be upwardly mobile. No one even thinks about the state of those on the lower rungs of life. Amma is reminded of a story. A poor woman was engaged as a domestic worker in a rich man's house. Her husband had died and her

7 This and the subsequent chapters (until 'Christmas') contain some of the different messages that Amma gave in conjunction with various public holidays and festivals over the years.

daughter was handicapped. She would take her handicapped daughter with her to work. The rich man had a daughter, who loved the handicapped daughter dearly. She would affectionately feed her sweets and tell her stories.

But her father did not like this and scolded his daughter. "Don't play with that child. Why do you want to carry that handicapped girl around with you?" Hearing this, his daughter remained silent. The rich man thought it was because his daughter did not have a playmate that she was spending all her time with the domestic worker's child. So, one day, he brought home his friend's daughter. The rich man's daughter smiled at the girl and spent some time talking to her. Then, she carried the servant's daughter and started caressing her affectionately. Seeing this, the father asked, "Daughter, don't you like the friend I brought here?"

His daughter said, "Father, I like the girl. But let me tell you something. Even if I don't love her, many others will. But the domestic worker's daughter has no one else to love her."

Like the rich man's daughter, we too must try to cultivate a kind heart. We must strive to gain a heart that yearns to serve others for the welfare of the world. Many people close their eyes and meditate, hoping their third eye will open. But we must never close our eyes to the problems of the world in the name of spirituality. We become spiritually liberated only when we are able to see ourselves in all beings while our eyes are open. Perfection is being able to love and serve others, seeing ourselves in them.

There is nothing wrong with wanting to scale the ladder of success in the world. But let us not forget to develop a compassionate heart. Children, may the New Year offer you this opportunity.

2

Children, the previous year passed after gifting you many sweet memories and bitter experiences. This New Year, let us awaken the memories of love, friendship and happiness, and gain inspiration from them. At the same time, let us forgive and forbear the experiences of failure and hatred, and move on.

Life is like a garden, where one can find withered leaves and dry twigs. The fallen leaves decompose and serve as fertilizers for new shoots. Similarly, we can transform the mistakes and miseries of the past into manure for our growth. Then, we can embrace life enthusiastically and make it joyful.

Instead of brooding over the mistakes and failures of the past, let us open a new chapter in our life. Amma is reminded of a story. Once, in the middle of a speech, a Guru cracked a joke. Hearing it, the audience roared with laughter. A second later, the Guru repeated the joke. This time, only a few people laughed. When the Guru repeated the joke yet again, no one laughed. Smiling, the Guru said, "We are unable to laugh if we hear the same joke again and again. So, what meaning is there in brooding over our mistake and lamenting over it repeatedly? Instead of shackling the mind to the past, move ahead!"

The New Year is an opportunity to clear the weeds from the heart and to sow the seeds of goodness. Let us forget what ought to be forgotten, forgive what ought to be forgiven, and step into the New Year with fresh hope and love. Life becomes blessed when we can find happiness in the happiness of another instead of catering to our own selfishness. We waste a lot of money on bad habits and luxuries. If we can use that money on people who cannot afford even one meal or for the suffering, we can spread the light of goodness in their lives. If we succeed in bringing about such a transformation in our lives this New Year, this whole year will become filled with newness. Then life will become meaningful.

When we give up hatred and selfishness, a New Year of love and unity will dawn within us. Then, we can usher in a society filled with peace and prosperity.

3

Children, the dawn of a New Year fills our heart with joy, hope and enthusiasm. Amma prays that this year will usher in peace and prosperity into the hearts and lives of everyone.

There was a lot of sorrow and suffering in the world last year. Thousands of lives were sacrificed on the altar of terrorism. The world has yet to recover from the mass murders that took place recently.[8] We seem to have forgotten the language of peace and contentment.

A snake's poison is in its mouth whereas a scorpion's is in its tail. Only man carries poison in his heart. Until this poison is removed, there will be no reprieve from most of the problems we face today. When a person acts viciously, we say that he behaves like an animal. But in saying so, we are unknowingly insulting animals, who never attack anyone out of hatred or vengeance.

8 Amma was alluding to the terrorist attacks that took place in Paris in November 2015.

Some ask, how can we continue smiling amidst so much sorrow and suffering? True, it is difficult to remain happy under such tragic circumstances. But how can remaining stuck in sorrow and depression help us? It cannot! If we lose hope and faith in the future, we will be like a bird whose wings have been clipped. We will never be able to soar into the skies of life.

To make life meaningful, we must observe five things: One, we must never miss any opportunity to help others. This will not only give joy to them, it will also awaken joy in our own hearts. Two, we must avoid slandering others and gossiping about them. Doing so will only agitate our minds and that of our listeners. All good and evil start with a word. Three, we must ensure that there is no break in our worship, prayers and other spiritual practices. Daily worship and spiritual practice are needed to remove the impurities that seep into the mind every day and to infuse the mind with peace and joy. Four, we must listen to and assimilate the essence of a satsaṅg every day, even if it is for a short time. The ideal satsaṅg is the presence of a living spiritual master and listening to scriptural texts. Five, we must daily open our hearts and pray to God to bless us with pure hearts and the strength to do good. Such humility and devotion are necessary for spiritual growth. If we observe these five things, the New Year will definitely make us joyful.

4

Children, each day of the New Year is actually a new page in the Book of Life. Let us fill these pages with the pen of wisdom, using the ink of effort.

Infinite strength and love reside within us. We must offer them to the world in the form of good deeds; otherwise, that strength and love will be wasted. People with compassionate hearts not only give joy and happiness to others. They experience happiness themselves and become an inspiration for others.

A girl won a competition. The prize was two tickets to the USA. When she went on stage to receive the prize, the presenter asked her, "Are you pleased to win the first prize?"

She replied, "Yes, but I would be happier if you could give me the money for the tickets instead."

The presenter asked her, "Why do you ask for the money instead of the tickets? Don't you wish to visit the US?"

"It's not that," she said. "My mom is a nurse. Last week, when I went to the hospital with her, I met a girl of my age. Within minutes, we became close friends. She spoke to me for a long time about her dreams for the future. Later, when I shared what she said with my mother, my mom told me sadly, 'That girl is suffering from an advanced stage of cancer. Her parents don't have money for the treatment. Unless she is transferred to a super-specialty hospital where she can receive the best treatment, the girl does not have long to live.' I cannot forget her innocent face, her hopes and desires, and her faith that she will soon be healed. With the prize money, she can get proper treatment. True victory for me would be snatching her from the jaws of death."

Hearing her words, the organizers of the competition immediately agreed to give her money in lieu of the tickets.

This New Year, let us pledge that we will not go to sleep without doing one deed that gives joy or solace to someone. It does not matter if we cannot do great deeds. A kind word, a loving smile, a heart willing to listen to the sorrow of others—these are more than enough. This New Year, let us aim to create a world full of joy and peace.

5

Children, the New Year has arrived, bringing new expectations with it. Each New Year is like a new page in the Book of Life. It is we who decide what to write in it. We can pen notes on love, peace and compassion, or fill it with expressions of hatred, selfishness and laziness.

If our finger pokes our eye, we will not chop off the finger. Instead, we will use the same finger to caress the eye because we know that both the eye and finger are parts of our own body. Similarly, if we see everyone as a part of God, we can only act with compassion. Not only that, just as we forget and forgive our own faults, we will be able to forget and forgive the faults of others.

A husband and wife fought over something and stopped talking to each other. Neither of them took the first step to initiate a reconciliation. Even after a week, neither of them was willing to talk to the other. Unable to bear the rift any longer, the husband started searching every nook and cranny of the house as if he had lost something valuable. The wife watched as he went down on his knees to peer under the sofa, climbed on chairs and tabletops, and searched high and low. Unable to control her curiosity, his wife asked, "What are you looking for?"

This was what the husband had been waiting to hear. He said, "Your sweet voice!" Hearing his loving reply, the wife forgot all her differences with him and smiled at him. If we can forget and forgive each other, peace and happiness will fill our lives.

This New Year, let us vow not to go to sleep without doing at least one deed that gives joy or solace to someone. Let us send a loving letter or email to those who are angry with us. It will help to douse the fire of anger burning within them and kindle joy instead. Let us also not forget to give thanks to our near and dear ones. Such acts bring newness to the New Year. Through such good deeds, we gain a new lease on life.

This New Year, may our hearts become free of anxiety, fear and hatred. May we become calm and peaceful and filled with compassion. May the sun of wisdom dawn in our heads. May we be able to make this New Year a blessed one with deeds arising from love and compassion.

6

Children, when New Year dawns, a thousand flowers blossom in the garden of our heart. A thousand colors burst forth. New hopes and expectations fill the heart. Newness is always captivating. Yet, in reality, all newness is within. A child looks upon the world with so much joy. Everything is new for him because there is newness and love in him. Because of these qualities, beauty also resides in him. Hence, he finds beauty and joy in every object of the world. If we can safeguard these qualities—the freshness of the mind and the attitude of love for the world—every day will become a New Year filled with uniqueness.

Actually, each day and each moment of the year ought to be new for us. Like a newly blossomed rose, we must be able to approach each moment of life with freshness and new hope.

The New Year reminds us of the flow of time. We might be able to regain anything we have lost but time once gone can never be reclaimed. So, the New Year is not just for losing ourselves in revelry. It is an opportunity to awaken wisdom and discernment.

The New Year is known as *Putuvarṣam*[9] in Malayāḷam. The New Year bears with it the coolness and vitality of new rains. For the young, it brings flowers of hope and expectations whereas for the grown-ups, it brings the fruits of new responsibilities. We always dream of a better tomorrow. It is these dreams that give color and fragrance to life even in the midst of sorrow. We must never give up this hope and optimistic faith.

The dawn of the New Year is an opportunity for new beginnings. It is an auspicious time to let go of sad and bitter memories and to take a new step forward. We must be willing to learn lessons from the past and, in its light, make changes in our life and habits.

Life is like a garden. It is natural for leaves to wither and for flowers to wilt. Only if we clean up the undergrowth of dead and fallen leaves and flowers can we enjoy the beauty of a garden filled with fresh blossoms and green shoots. Likewise, let us let go of the turbulent thoughts and emotions of the past. Let us forgive what ought to be forgiven and forget what ought to be forgotten. Let us embrace life with new vigor.

9 'Putu' means new. 'Varṣam' can mean either year or shower.

Viṣu

Children, every Viṣu[10] comes with the message of happiness and prosperity. *Viṣukkaṇi*[11] marks our entry into the dawn of a new year. The Viṣukkaṇi is a miniature portrait of the universe. The Viṣukkaṇi includes books, which represent material knowledge; the lamp, which symbolizes spiritual wisdom; as well as fruits, vegetables and the like, which signify prosperity.

When Viṣu dawns, the mothers or grandmothers in each home will awaken the children and other family members, cover their eyes, and lead them to the altar. After placing them before the image of God, the mothers or grandmothers will remove their hands from in front of the family members' eyes. Opening their eyes, the children will see the beautiful form of the Lord and the Viṣukkaṇi, suffused with golden light from the lamp. At this, their minds will be filled with devotion and joy. This is their 'capital' for the year. Creator and creation come together in the Viṣukkaṇi. If we can reverentially behold the divine

10 Popular Hindu festival celebrated in Kerala and which coincides with the spring equinox and is celebrated as the New Year.

11 'That which is first seen on Viṣu.' It refers to the arrangement of items that are considered auspicious, and which are placed at the altar. Traditionally, the elders in the family light the lamp at the altar on the morning of Viṣu. The others in the family are led there with their eyes closed. When they open their eyes, the first thing they behold is the Viṣukkaṇi.

consciousness dwelling in everyone, life will be peaceful and joyful. This is the message of Viṣu.

Sanātana Dharma teaches us that Creator and creation are not two, but one. Therefore, whenever we see any object in creation, we are beholding God, the Creator of everything. It is important to cultivate this remembrance and awareness. We use every item in the Viṣukkaṇi in daily life. Using them must awaken the remembrance of God in us.

Amma is reminded of a story. Surdās, who was born blind, was once walking to Vṛndāvan. On the way, he was befriended by a young boy, who became his guide. Surdās found the young boy's talk, jokes and mischiefs captivating. As they were nearing Vṛndāvan, Surdās experienced an epiphany. He realized that the boy was Kṛṣṇa Himself. With deep fervor, Surdās pulled the boy to him with both hands and embraced him. But Kṛṣṇa slipped away from Surdās's grip and ran off. Surdās said, "O Kṛṣṇa, you might be able to break free from my hands, but you will never be able to run away from my heart!"

Pleased with Surdās's devotion, Kṛṣṇa said, "I shall bless you with vision." Thus, Surdās gained the gift of sight. With his eyes, he drank in the beautiful form of Kṛṣṇa. Suddenly, Surdās exclaimed, "O Kṛṣṇa, take away my eyesight! I don't wish to see anything more with these eyes that have seen your beautiful form!" Surdās became blind again. But with his inner eye, he saw Kṛṣṇa everywhere, all the time. A true devotee is always in the presence of God. He always perceives the unity underlying the diversity of the universe. Loving, serving and worshipping everyone and everything becomes second nature to him.

The message of Viṣu is no different. Every festival is about sharing, which arises from love and friendship. Real beauty arises from a union of hearts. Let us welcome such a beautiful and joyful Viṣu.

Tiruvōṇam

1

Children, Tiruvōṇam[12] is a festival that celebrates mutual love and sharing. Human beings, nature, birds and animals join in the festivities. The youth, women and the elderly play their part. Even flowers and butterflies take part in this joyous festival celebrated all over the land. Thus, in all respects, Tiruvōṇam is a grand celebration of love and unity.

Our ancestors used to say that we must partake of the Ōṇam feast, even if it means selling off our property. There is a hidden message in this saying. Mutual love and happiness have a higher place in life than wealth and property. This does not mean that we should not strive to earn money or that wealth is not necessary, but that we must understand that they will not be with us forever. But many of us forget this. In a bid to amass wealth, we forgo food and sleep, compete with each other, and stop expressing love to our family and friends. Our only thoughts are of work and money.

We ought to love people and use objects, but today, we love objects and use people. Whether phone or computer, we love objects so much that we spend hours with them. But we don't spare any time to speak to, look at, or even smile at our family

12 The last day of Ōṇam , which is Kerala's biggest festival, occurring in the month of Ciṅṅam (August – September).

members at home, never mind the neighbors or other people in our community. If this continues to persist, family ties will unravel, and social harmony will be disrupted.

Once, a husband told his wife, "I'm going to start a big business. Through this business, we will earn a fortune in the future!"

Hearing this, the wife said, "Aren't we rich already?"

"How so? Right now, we only have enough to live frugally, don't we?"

The wife replied, "My dear, you're with me and I'm with you. When we have each other, what do we lack?"

Hearing his wife's loving words, the man hugged her affectionately.

Children, love is our true wealth; it is what life truly is. If we have no love for each other, our life will be a hell, no matter how much wealth we possess.

We can begin to live by the principle of Tiruvōṇam only when we restore love and happiness to life. May the memories of Ōṇam help us cultivate such noble values in life.

2

Children, Ōṇam is an occasion for fun and celebration. But this year, Ōṇam has come at a time of intense sorrow and distress.[13] Many have died; many have lost their families; and many have lost all that they owned. This is the time to act upon the true message of Ōṇam: unity, love and co-operation. Above all, Ōṇam is a celebration of human love and sharing. It is an opportunity

13 *Amma is alluding to the severe floods that affected Kerala in August 2018.*

to strengthen the bonds of love. It's a great relief to see the people of Kerala and the citizens of India wholeheartedly living the message of Ōṇam.

After a young woman got married, she found her mother-in-law quick-tempered and obstinate. Soon, the mother-in-law's behavior became intolerable. The daughter-in-law told her older brother, a traditional healer, "I've had enough of my mother-in-law! I need to get rid of her somehow!"

Her brother said, "If she dies suddenly, suspicions will be aroused. I'll give you a medicine. You must mix small amounts of it into her food and give it to her. Within six months, you'll be rid of her. But be careful that she doesn't suspect anything. Behave very lovingly to her and try to obey her as much as you can."

The sister agreed and started doing as her brother instructed: she began to mix the medicine in her mother-in-law's food before serving it to her. The daughter-in-law also started behaving lovingly to her. Within four months, the atmosphere in the house changed completely. Seeing how loving her daughter-in-law had become, the mother-in-law became loving to her. The two of them began to appreciate each other more and more.

One day, the daughter-in-law told her older brother, "It was a mistake to poison my mother-in-law's food. She's a good woman and very loving to me. Please give me an antidote to the poison."

Her brother laughed and said, "That wasn't poison! It was a tonic to boost her health. I knew that the problems were caused by your behavior. My plan was actually a ruse to make you love and serve her. Now, she has started loving you in return."

Similarly, we must try to change ourselves instead of changing others. If we give love, we will definitely get love in return. We just need to be patient.

At present, God is in the form of Vāmana (a small boy) within us. We must nourish him through our love, sacrifice, spiritual practices and compassion to the world so that he becomes Trivikrama.[14] We ought to be able to love and serve others, seeing God in them. Only then will Ōṇam truly become Ōṇam.

3

Children, Ōṇam commemorates the beautiful egalitarianism of a bygone era. Mahābali is considered an ideal role model because he ruled with the interests of his subjects at heart and because he never abandoned truth and righteousness even in the most trying of times. A philanthropist, Mahābali never swerved from the path of truth and dharma. As a result, he attained great prosperity and pre-eminence and became emperor of the three worlds.

Many people criticize Lord Viṣṇu for pushing Mahābali down into the netherworld; they say that the act was unrighteous. But there is no mention in any of the Purāṇas of the Lord shoving

14 An allusion to the famous legend behind Ōṇam. Mahābali was a benevolent monarch, who prided himself on his generosity. To humble him and teach him that everything belongs to God, Lord Viṣṇu appeared in the guise of Vāmana, a small boy, and asked Mahābali for land that could be measured by three paces. Mahābali was amused by this seemingly insignificant request and acceded to the request. Vāmana grew in stature. With the first step, he covered the whole earth. With the second, he covered the heavens. Seeing that there was nowhere else for Vāmana to place his third step, Mahābali humbly bowed down and offered his own head. This signifies the surrender of the ego.

Bali down into the netherworld. According to the *Bhāgavatam*, the Lord made Mahābali the ruler of a realm more exalted than heaven, and the Lord himself became his guard.

Even though Mahābali knew that he had lost everything, he stood firmly by the truth. He offered not only his wealth but also himself to the Lord. He humbly bowed down and offered his head to the Lord. Through complete surrender, Mahābali gained everything. In return for his whole-hearted surrender, the Lord bestowed on Mahābali everlasting fame. This land has been graced by Lord Kṛṣṇa's birth and Lord Rāma's rule. Yet, people still long for Mahābali to rule them. Why? It is because, though an *asura* (anti-god) by birth, he found a place in the hearts of people through his actions and sacrifice.

All of us long for egalitarianism, which characterized Mahābali's times. All of us want to live in a society that is righteous, auspicious and prosperous. Why is it that, though all of us share this desire for a just and equitable society, our country hasn't become like that? Whatever the goal, we must pay a price for it. To get a good job, we must forgo sleep and study hard. To reap a good harvest, we must sow the seeds at the right time and nourish them with sufficient water and fertilizer. Similarly, if we sincerely wish to see a positive transformation in society, we must put forth the right effort. It's not enough just to wish. We must also be prepared to work with discipline and to endure hardship.

May every action we do during this Ōṇam be an offering for the welfare of society. May our hearts be filled with love and compassion, just like the floral decorations marking the celebrations. May the resolve to create a new life based on righteousness and remembrance of the Divine be the new clothes we wear this Ōṇam. May the Ōṇam games remind us that what gives us joy must also make others happy. May we all be infused with the spirit of kinship behind the Ōṇam games, which celebrate unity, disregarding differences in caste or creed. May we thus forget all kinds of differences and become of one heart, united in love and joy.

4

Children, we celebrate Ōṇam to commemorate a bygone era, when there was no starvation or poverty and when everyone lived in love and unity. We all want and hope that such good times can last forever. This is a noble wish. Today's wishes become tomorrow's reality.

The legend of Ōṇam teaches us many noble lessons. Although Mahābali had many sterling qualities, the 'I' sense in him was very strong. He egoistically believed, "I am the emperor of the three worlds! See how generous I am!" All the wealth that we amass will leave us today or tomorrow. We ought to cultivate the attitude that, "Everything is His. It is only by His power that I am able to serve as His instrument and give generously to others." Only then will we gain the full benefit of our noble deeds. The Lord showed Mahābali how two of His footsteps could cover the three worlds. In this way, the Lord destroyed the ego of Mahābali, who became ready to surrender his very life to Him. Thus, Bali was elevated to immortality. The Lord Himself became his guard. Where there is surrender, the Lord's protection is certain.

Ōṇam is a time of togetherness and sharing. All the relatives gather in the ancestral home and share their joys. Neighbors prepare delectable snacks and share them with each other. What we give others comes back to us a hundredfold.

When Kṛṣṇa was a young boy in Ambāḍi, he once heard someone calling out, "Ripe mangoes for sale!" When he ran out to look, Kṛṣṇa saw an old woman walking with a basket of mangoes on her head. He ran up to the old woman and held out his hand for a mango. Unwilling to give too many mangoes away for free, the old woman picked out a small mango, gave it to Kṛṣṇa, and walked away.

She wasn't able to sell many mangoes that day. She returned home, despondent, put down the basket, and went to sleep.

The next day, she got ready to go out again to sell the mangoes. When she looked into the basket, she was stunned. There was a golden mango nestled among the other mangoes. It was the same size as the one she had given little Kṛṣṇa. She wistfully thought, "If only I had given the Lord all the mangoes!" Whenever we give, we are actually gaining.

During Ōṇam , children collect flowers from various plants to make colorful floral decorations. When the flowers are of different colors and sizes, the floral decoration becomes especially lovely and evokes a refreshing ambience of beauty. When each flower loses its individuality, its 'I' sense, something new and beautiful is created. When we get rid of our ego, our inner beauty and goodness become manifest. Each one of us is a flower in the floral decoration that is society. Our devotion to God is the sweet nectar in those flowers. If our individual minds can become one collective mind filled with devotion to God, we can create a beautiful world. True beauty lies in the oneness of hearts. This is the message of Ōṇam.

5

Children, *Ciṅṅam* (in August) comes with the message of clear skies, clean nature and auspiciousness after a wet and gloomy *Karkaṭaka* (July). Golden Ōṇam is the *tilak* (mark) on the forehead of golden Ciṅṅam. It is Kerala's grandest festival and a symbol of an auspicious tomorrow.

Creation always takes place in the mind first. If the mind conceives of something noble, it will become a reality before long. This is the relevance of optimistic faith. Such faith can be seen in the legend of Tiruvōṇam: the enthusiastic belief that the prosperity marking the reign of Mahābali will return.

It is optimistic faith that makes life beautiful. Even when defeat is staring at us in the face, if we try just a little harder, we will definitely succeed. The ECG (electrocardiogram) shows highs and lows. If we don't see them, it means that the person has died. Highs and lows are the nature of life.

Ōṇam presents an idealized portrait of the relationship between rulers and the ruled. Mahābali ruled with only the welfare of his people in mind. His subjects adored him. Ōṇam unfolds before us the panorama of the unity, love and equality among them.

Ōṇam also conveys the message that we need to restore and strengthen human relationships. Ōṇam becomes Ōṇam only when we do so. There might be times in our life when others badly need our love and help. If we can give them love and assistance then, our life becomes so much more blessed.

There is a belief that Mahābali comes to earth on Ōṇam to inquire after the well-being of his subjects. The principle behind this belief is that we must awaken from the sleep of selfishness and perceive society through the eyes of Mahābali. What makes life blissful are the small acts of love and respect that we show our fellow beings. When each one of us thinks about what we can do to make others happy, joy will naturally fill everyone's hearts.

It is customary to wear new clothes on Tiruvōṇam. Let us also try to put on the new robes of resolutions made for the uplift of society. We compete with each other to make the biggest floral decorations. At the same time, let us also adorn our heart with floral decorations made from the blossoms of love, patience, sacrifice, humility and other noble qualities. Let us try to enlarge the circle of compassion. Then, life itself will become a grand Ōṇam celebration.

6

Children, Ōṇam is a celebration of our culture, a festival commemorating sweet memories and anticipating great expectations. Man and nature take part in it equally. But it is also a time to reflect on the true message of Ōṇam.

Tiruvōṇam proclaims the great truth that the one who surrenders everything gains everything. It also conveys the message of sacrifice. It is a call to rise up from the level of selfishness and egoism to the level of humility. It exhorts us to bring back the golden period when truth, righteousness, love, equality, charity and compassion ruled the day.

There once lived a cobbler in a village. For many years, he harbored a deep desire to go on a pilgrimage. He toiled hard and went without food to save money for his journey. One day, the aroma of beans being roasted came wafting from the neighboring hut. The cobbler's pregnant wife wanted to have bean curry. The cobbler went next door and asked for a little curry. The woman of the house said "You may take it if you wish. But it is very impure. We've all been going without food for a week. When we couldn't bear the hunger any longer, my husband collected some beans growing in the nearby cemetery. This curry is made from those beans."

Hearing this, the cobbler's face turned pale. He thought, "It's not right for me to save money to go on a pilgrimage when my neighbors have been starving for a week." He went back home, took out all his savings, and gave them to the neighbors. Although they refused to accept the money at first, they gave in to the cobbler's loving insistence.

That night, the cobbler had a vision of the Lord in his dreams. The Lord said, "O son, you need not go on any pilgrimage to get my darśan. You have already acquired the merits of going on a pilgrimage. I am pleased with you!"

Only if we can cultivate sacrifice and an awareness of the right values, like the cobber did, can we assimilate the message of Ōṇam in our lives.

During Ōṇam, we make floral decorations with many varieties and colors of flowers. Each color represents our pursuit of wealth and desires. Only when these diverse colors come together within the mandala of the floral decoration will the floral decoration become beautiful. The circle in which the flowers are arranged is a symbol of *dharma* (righteousness). The floral decoration of life becomes beautiful only when the blossoms of our goals and desires are contained within the circle of dharma. If so, our life will become beautiful, brilliant and blissful.

Śivarātri

1

Children, 'Śiva' means 'auspiciousness.' God is the abode of all things auspicious. Auspiciousness prevails only in a place that is vibrant with thoughts of God. During Śivarātri,[15] the practice of fasting is given a lot of importance. In truth, every night is Śivarātri for those who forgo food and sleep to remember God while everyone else has eaten well and is sleeping. But not everyone has so much discernment and dispassion. It is to create such an opportunity for us at least once a year that we celebrate Śivarātri.

Food and mind are related to each other. If we fast and reflect on God, the mind easily becomes one-pointed. It is said that the gods fasted and prayed all night for the well-being of Śiva, who had imbibed the deadly Kālakūṭa poison. Śiva is within us. We observe the vow of fasting on Śivarātri so that the poison of Māyā[16] does not affect the inner Śiva.

The Ganges is said to be in Lord Śiva's matted locks. The Purāṇas say that the outer Ganges has the power to destroy sin. The sacred Ganges resides within us also. When yogis attain perfection through meditation, the pure Ganges rises within them. The Ganges here is a reference to the *kuṇḍalinī*

15 *Literally, 'Night of Śiva.' A festival celebrated in honor of Lord Śiva.*

16 *The illusory nature of the world*

śakti.[17] When the kuṇḍalinī śakti travels from the *mūlādhāra* and reaches the *sahasrāra*, *amṛta* (the ambrosia of bliss) gushes forth. Its cascading flow is the Ganges. This is the principle behind the saying that Śiva has hidden the Ganges in his matted locks. It doesn't mean that Śiva has a secret second wife!

Some wonder if Śiva, who lives in the crematory ground, isn't primitive. Saying that Śiva lives in the crematory ground is indicative of a certain principle. The cemetery is where all the worldly desires of man and the body, which is the means of fulfilling them, are burnt to ashes. It is here that Śiva dances in bliss. When the intense attachment to the body is reduced to ash in the fire of knowledge, bliss naturally wells up within us.

Śiva is dispassionate. When we hear the word dispassion, we might think it means aversion to the world. But that is not what it means. Dispassion is the lack of attachment to anything. If we do not cultivate true dispassion, we will rely on the words of others for our happiness. Our life becomes a plaything in the hands of others. Dispassion brings us true freedom. If we are truly dispassionate, no object in the world will be able to inhibit our natural happiness. It is this principle that Śiva, who is adorned with ash and who lives in the crematory ground, teaches us. Children, may Śivarātri help to awaken in us the knowledge and dispassion that shines gloriously in Lord Śiva.

---

17 Spiritual power, personified as a snake coiled in the mūlādhāra cakra, a psychic center of spiritual power located near the coccyx, at the base of the spine. During the process of spiritual awakening, the snake of spiritual power rises through the spinal column and ultimately reaches the sahasrāra, or crown cakra, envisaged as a thousand-petalled lotus; this is when one attains spiritual enlightenment.

2

Children, festivals and group observances of vows play a key role in turning our minds to God. When many people gather to contemplate on and pray to God, uplifting thought waves are produced. It might be more difficult to prevail over negative thought waves through solitary prayer. But when we engage in group worship, the very environment becomes conducive for turning the mind Godward. As a result, people's disposition to spirituality becomes stronger.

The real aim of festivals lies beyond the festive excitement that lasts for a few days. It is to deepen our predisposition to worshipping and contemplating the Divine constantly. This is also the aim of Śivarātri, a major festival. Śivarātri reminds us to forget all other thoughts, immerse ourselves in the remembrance of God, and realize the ultimate goal of human life.

Śivarātri is a festival of renunciation and austerity. It is customary to fast during the day and to stay awake the whole night, dedicating it to prayer and bhajans. Usually, no one is willing to give up food and sleep. But Śivarātri inspires even an ordinary person to awaken the love of God lying dormant within them, and to forgo food and sleep in the name of religious penance.

One evening, a milkmaid of Vṛndāvan went to Nanda's[18] house to get some fire to light her own lamp. She was also hoping to see infant Kṛṣṇa there. She reached the house and brought the wick in the lamp she was holding close to the lamp there. That was when she noticed infant Kṛṣṇa lying in the cradle. Her attention became riveted on him. She did not realize that instead of the

18 Nanda was Lord Kṛṣṇa's foster-father.

wick, she had stretched her hand into the fire and did not feel the flames starting to burn her fingers.

In the meantime, noticing that the milkmaid had been gone for a long time, her mother went in search of her daughter and reached Nanda's house. What she saw was unbelievable! Her daughter was standing with her hand in the fire and gazing intently at Kṛṣṇa. Seeing her hand aflame, the mother ran to her, yanked her hand out of the fire, and exclaimed, "Daughter, what are you doing?"

That was when the milkmaid came back to her senses. The sight of Kṛṣṇa had made her forget everything else. She had become transported to the heights of devotion and did not feel the slightest pain. This story shows us that when love for a noble goal awakens within, we will gain the strength to overcome the limitations of body and mind.

May we be able to observe the vows associated with Śivarātri, and thus nourish our love for God, and become worthy of the blessings of Lord Śiva, the very embodiment of renunciation, austerity and wisdom.

3

Children, festivals like Śivarātri are opportunities to awaken our love for God. More than a festival, Śivarātri denotes the observance of vows that emphasize renunciation, austerity and self-control. On Śivarātri, it is customary to fast throughout the day and to spend the night in prayer and bhajans. Staying awake does not mean just keeping our eyes open but awakening to the awareness of the Self. The way to it is through awareness of our own thoughts, words and deeds.

There are many legends associated with Śivarātri. One of them is the churning of the milky ocean. The milky ocean represents the mind. When the milky ocean was churned, the first thing that emerged was the Kāḷakūṭa poison. To protect the world from it, Lord Śiva swallowed the poison. The Kāḷakūṭa poison represents lust, anger, egoism and other negative tendencies of the mind. We can overcome them with patience and discernment. Doing so will be propitious both for ourselves and the world.

Amma is reminded of a story. A famous professor gave a talk. The next day, he received a letter pointing out a few mistakes he had made in the previous day's talk. When he read it, the professor became furious, and thought, "I shall teach whoever wrote this letter a lesson!" Fuming, he penned a response to the letter. In it, he harshly rebuked and criticized the writer. By the time he finished writing the letter, it was late and the post office was closed. He kept the letter on the table and went to sleep. As soon as he woke up, he read the letter he had written and thought, "The tone of the letter is severe. Is that necessary? I could tone it down a bit." He softened the language. When he reread the letter, he felt that he could make it milder yet. So, he rewrote the letter. While doing so, he began reflecting on his talk and realized that he had indeed made some mistakes. So, he wrote, "I would like to meet you," and suggested a time and place for the meeting. When they met, he realized that the critic was a woman. They went to a restaurant and had a cup of coffee. They discussed the topic and became friends. Their friendship eventually culminated in marriage.

When he patiently strove to understand the person whom he was angry with and had hated at first, he was able to accept her point of view and draw closer to her. What happened? Sleep cleared his mind and calmed him down. He gained more inner clarity. That was when he realized that choosing not to react instinctively in anger had been a wise move. This is the greatness of patience and self-control. We must train ourselves to exercise self-control in all situations and to analyze matters patiently. If we can do so, we can move ahead in life and do good to society.

Just as Lord Śiva was willing to ingest poison for the sake of the world, we must also be willing to give up at least a little of our selfishness and egoism. One who is willing to bear afflictions and sacrifice his or her own comfort for the sake of humanity becomes Lord Śiva; i.e. more spiritually evolved than others. Children, may you have the strength and blessings to become that.

4

Children, Lord Śiva is also known as Āśutōṣ. It means one who is easily pleased. It does not mean that the Lord will fulfill all our prayers immediately. If our attitude is correct, the Lord will be pleased at once. The best prayer we can offer the Lord is a heart filled with devotion and gratitude, without desiring or demanding anything. When He sees such innocence and selflessness, the Lord will be pleased right away. Among all the forms of worship, worship done with a pure heart and a one-pointed mind is dearest to the Lord.

Once, a king who was a devotee of Śiva, built a magnificent temple to the Lord. He made elaborate preparations for its consecration. The night before the consecration ceremony, the king dreamt of the Lord, who said, "I am pleased with your devotion and worship. But I cannot attend the consecration ceremony as I have to attend another consecration ceremony. That temple and the preparations there are much more magnificent than yours." The Lord then disclosed to the king the name of the devotee who built the temple and the village in which he lived. The king woke up that very moment and thought, "A temple that is superior to the one I built? I must see it for myself!"

The king set out with his entourage and went to the village mentioned by the Lord, but did not see any new temple there. He found his way to the devotee's house — it was a thatched hut. Looking inside, he saw a man in rags meditating. He thought, "Is this the Lord's foremost devotee?" The king felt both amazement and contempt. He prayed to Lord Śiva to clear his doubts. At once, the king was able to see inside the mind of the rustic villager.

The king saw a wondrous temple inside the devotee's heart. The devotee was performing *abhiṣēka* (ceremonial bathing) to Lord Śiva, with the sacred waters of the Ganges, which filled thousands of pots. The temple resounded with the clarion calls of conches and the reverberant chanting of mantras. Many sages, gods and goddesses were present. Lord Śiva manifested Himself clearly within the Śivaliṅga[19] and was blessing everyone present. Seeing this, the king's pride and arrogance left him. He realized how lofty the yōgī's devotion was and fell devoutly at his feet.

We must enshrine God in our heart. The mind ought to become one pointed. Not knowing this, we give undue

19 Literally, 'emblem of Śiva.' An abstract representation of the beginningless and endless nature of the Divine.

importance to external rituals and decorations. God will shine constantly in a heart that is pure and overflowing with devotion to God.

Navarātri

1

Children, *Navarātri*[20] is a festival dedicated to the worship of Jagadambā, the Mother of the Universe, who is the very embodiment of *śakti* (primordial power). During this festival, Dēvī is worshipped primarily in the three forms of Durgā, Lakṣmī and Saraswatī. These three forms of the Goddess signify the creation, sustenance and destruction of the universe. Because Dēvī embodies all three powers, She is also known as Tryambikā. The Navarātri celebration symbolizes the annihilation of the *tāmasic* (dull) and *asuric* (demonic) tendencies within us, as a result of which one is uplifted to the state of perfection.

Traditionally, young children undergo the *Vidyārambham* ceremony on *Vijayadaśamī*.[21] The Sanskrit word for alphabet, '*akṣara*,' means 'imperishable.' God is the only one who is imperishable. Therefore, children are first made to write '*Hari śrī gaṇapatayē namaḥ*,' the names of God, during the Vidyārambham ceremony. Vidyārambham reminds us that it is not enough to acquire worldly knowledge. All knowledge ought to lead us

20 Literally, 'nine nights.' A festival honoring the Divine Mother.

21 Vijayadaśamī marks the 10th day (*daśamī*) of, or day after, Navarātri. It denotes the victory (*vijaya*) of good over evil. Vidyārambham, literally 'commencement of education,' is a ritual to initiate young children into learning.

to God. Otherwise, literacy will create *rākṣasas* (demons)! The rākṣasas had knowledge but they were slaves to their ego. Hence, their knowledge and skills created only sorrow and suffering for others. Not only that, from the Puranic stories, we learn that their knowledge and skills eventually paved the way to their own destruction.

Compared to other conceptions of God, the Dēvī concept is much closer to nature. Dēvī is of the form of nature and She pervades all beings, moving and unmoving. For this very reason, one of the most important messages behind the Navarātri worship is to regard everything in the universe with love and respect. This is also the principle behind the *bomma-kolu*, a festive display of idols, dolls and figurines during Navarātri.

Navarātri helps to awaken in us an attitude of reverence towards everything. A tailor will place his needle for worshipping. He does not regard it as insignificant because it helps him earn a living. He sees it as God Himself. Likewise, any worker or artisan will put his or her tools in front of Jagadambā for worshipping.

In truth, there is nothing in the universe that is separate from God because goodness is intrinsic to every object. For someone who knows how to make use of every object, nothing is waste, everything is useful.

Amma remembers a story. Once, a Guru told his disciple, "Bring me something that's of absolutely no use in this world." The first thing the disciple saw was ash. Even though it looks useless at first glance, it has many uses. It can be used as fertilizer for plants and to scrub vessels clean. So, we cannot say that ash is completely useless. That's when a leaf floating on the backwaters caught his eye. Thinking that it was of no use, he went to pick it up. That is when he saw many ants on it. Even a dead leaf, which looked completely useless, could save the life of many ants. As he reflected once again, the disciple understood, "We cannot reject anything in the universe. If we see everything in its place, then we will accept it." Likewise, one who can see the goodness and presence of God in all beings, moving and unmoving, will definitely have a reverential attitude towards everything. Children, may this Navarātri celebration inspire my children to see the goodness in all.

2

Children, we worship God in the form of the Mother during Navarātri with the goal of attaining all the fortunes and the realization of the Truth. The tradition that is most prevalent is worshipping the Goddess in the three aspects of Durgā, Lakṣmī and Saraswatī. The principle behind Navarātri is of gradually rising above the mind's *tāmasic*, *rājasic* and *sāttvic* tendencies,[22] thus purifying the mind. Vijayadaśamī marks the successful completion of that worship. Vijayadaśamī is the most auspicious day to start new ventures. On this day, young children are initiated into the world of letters.

Jagadambā is the personification of love, compassion, affection and infinite patience. For this reason, the worship of Jagadambā is especially relevant in this day and age, which is marked by conflict, competition and a lack of love.

The highest goal of all spiritual practices and modes of worship is to see God in all beings, moving and unmoving. When

22 Tamas denotes lethargy; rajas signifies restlessness; and sattva indicates serenity.

we see God permeating the whole universe, we will be able to revere and love everyone.

Amma is reminded of a story. A young boy who was an ardent devotee of the Goddess intensely longed to see Her physical form. When he disclosed his desire to his Guru, the Guru said, "You will be able to see Dēvī, not in Her divine form, but in the form of an ordinary woman. Nevertheless, you will be able to identify Her by a mark. There will be a black mole on the big toe of Dēvī's right foot."

From that day onwards, whenever the boy saw a woman, he would look at her feet to see if there was a black mole on her big toe. Days and months passed, but the boy did not see such a mark. One day, when his mother came out to serve him food, the plate fell from her hand. When he bent down to pick up the plate, he noticed a black mole on the big toe of his mother's right foot. Overwhelmed by devotion, he fell prostrate before his mother.

If we wish to see God, we must first see Her in the people we associate with most closely: our own mother, father, teachers and friends. See and feel God in everyone we meet. Practice loving and respecting everyone. This is what we need to do. Then, we will gradually see God shining in everyone.

It is the remembrance of and surrender to God that makes our life blessed. Children, may you gain innocent love and the highest knowledge and thus make life blessed.

3

Children, Vijayadaśamī is the auspicious day when young children are initiated into the first letters of wisdom. Vijayadaśamī also marks the completion of the nine days of worshipping Dēvī as

Śakti. On that day, with the blessings of Saraswatī, the Goddess of Knowledge, young children write *'Hari śrī gaṇapatayē namaḥ'* and thus enter the world of knowledge. It is only when the child allows the Guru to hold its index finger that he or she is able to receive knowledge.[23] The index finger points to the mistakes of others and is therefore the symbol of the ego. By allowing the Guru to guide his index finger, the child surrenders his ego to the Guru.

One who has real knowledge will naturally be humble and see goodness in everyone. He or she will behave reverentially and respectfully towards others. Only the ego is our own creation; everything else is God's. It is the ego that we must surrender to God.

On Vijayadaśamī, both scholars and the unlettered start their learning anew by writing *'Hari śrī gaṇapatayē namaḥ.'* What makes knowledge perfect is the awareness of the limitations of what one has learned so far; the humility arising from the knowledge that there is so much more to learn; and the enthusiasm for new knowledge. Vijayadaśamī reminds us that we must uphold and maintain this humility, enthusiasm and dedication always.

On *Durgā Aṣṭami,*[24] we place our books, musical instruments and tools of work at the altar for worshipping, and take them back on Vijayadaśamī. The principle behind this practice is to surrender our very life to God and then take it back as His *prasād* (consecrated gift). Vijayadaśamī symbolizes starting life anew with the remembrance of and surrender to God.

23 An allusion to the Vidyārambham ceremony, in which the child sits in the lap of the Guru, who holds the child's right hand and uses the child's index finger to trace letters on a plate of grain.

24 Eighth day of Navarātri.

When we become victorious in life, we say, "My ability!" But when we fail, we say, "God is punishing me." That's not how we ought to think. We ought to feel that God is enabling us to act and thus think, "I am merely an instrument in His hands." Navarātri teaches us to awaken the awareness that all successes in life are as a result of God's blessings and His power, and reminds us not to forget ourselves in victory and become arrogant. What makes life blessed are remembrance of God and surrender to Him.

The message of Navarātri is that, more than material gains, we ought to progress step by step along the path of devotion and finally gain ultimate liberation. Jagadambā will remove all the mental impurities of those who have dedicated their lives to God-realization. She will destroy their ego and awaken within them the awareness of their own true Self.

4

Children, Navarātri is dedicated to the worship of Dēvī. We praise Dēvī as the personification of knowledge, power and prosperity. But above all, Dēvī is Mother, the very embodiment of compassion. The affection of all the mothers in the world is only an iota of Jagadambā's compassion. Dēvī lovingly nurtures all beings in this universe, like a mother taking care of her own children. Hence, Dēvī will readily forgive us for our mistakes and shortcomings and shower Her grace upon us.

There is a sweetness in a child's attitude to its mother. A baby sitting in its mother's lap fears nothing. When he is under his mother's protective wings, he enjoys himself, totally free of worries. Once we have gained that childlike and innocent heart, there is nothing else to gain.

There was a scholarly Brāhmin who was a devotee of Dēvī. She would go wherever he went. Though no one else could see Dēvī, the Brāhmin could see and talk to Her.

Once while traveling, he turned around to look for Dēvī but She was nowhere to be seen. He waited for some time, but Dēvī did not appear. He retraced his steps in search of Her. Then, he saw Dēvī sitting on a *pīṭham* (ceremonial seat) inside the hut of an outcaste. The outcaste had kept a sword and trident on the pīṭham, imagining Dēvī's presence there, and was worshipping Her and singing folk songs in praise of Her. All the while, Dēvī sat there smiling and enjoying his worship. When the pūjā ended, Dēvī approached the Brāhmin, who said, "O Mother! How could you spend so much time in the house of this outcaste and accept the worship of one who doesn't know either mantra or *tantra* (rituals of worship)? Please don't do this again!"

Hearing this, Dēvī smiled and said, "You still haven't understood me. I look at a person's heart. I don't distinguish between high and low. I will go to anyone who calls me with love. Innocent devotion is dearer to me than scriptural knowledge. As you still haven't understood this, I will no longer accompany you!" With those words, Dēvī disappeared. God distances Herself from a devotee when egoism and a sense of difference arise in his heart.

Sorrow and bondage come about when we see the universe as separate from God and indulge in our likes and dislikes, attractions and aversions. When we become aware that everything is the divine sport of the Divine Mother, who is the embodiment of power, our life also becomes a joyful play.

5

Children, the message of Navarātri is to worship and surrender to God. During Navarātri, we worship God in the form of the Mother with the goal of attaining material blessings and spiritual liberation.

To gain prosperity and success and to alleviate the sorrows and sufferings in life, we must worship God and do spiritual practices constantly. Occasions like Navarātri help us to take steps in that direction.

This world is like a supermarket. We can get anything here. But we must first understand what is worthy of desiring and acquiring. In truth, the only one worthy of taking to heart is God or Jagadambā. She is the ultimate refuge.

Navarātri is the time to purify our body and mind through vows. But first, we must remember God constantly. During Navarātri, devotees engage in practices such as performing pūjās to Dēvī and reciting the *Lalitā Sahasranāma*, *Dēvī Māhātmyam* and *Dēvī Bhāgavatam*. Equally important is *upavāsam* (fasting). 'Upavāsam' means to live near God, to direct all our sense organs Godward. We must also control our diet. Some devotees forsake food completely; others eat only once a day. We must at least give up fish and meat on those days.

We get energy not only from the food we eat but also from air and sunlight. When we reduce the intake of gross food, the ability of both the body and mind to absorb subtle food gets augmented. If we fast intelligently, we won't feel tired or exhausted. On the contrary, we will be more energized, focused and peaceful.

Vows are a practical means to subdue the vacillations of the mind. The more we bring the mind under control, the stronger it becomes. To build a boat, we need to bend the wood. To do this, the wood is heated. Vows are similar. They help us bring the mind under our control. Not only that, vows and observances make us befitting of the blessings of the deity we worship.

All the victories in life come because of God's blessings and power. Navarātri reminds us to awaken this awareness and not take pride in our successes. May our lives become blessed through true knowledge and proper efforts. May the Almighty bless us.

6

Children, the tradition of worshipping God as Mother has existed in India since time immemorial. Navarātri is the most propitious time for the worship of Dēvī.

Dēvī bestows prosperity and success. As She is in the form of a Mother, Dēvī showers Her blessings on Her children at once. A mother is responsible for protecting her children and raising them. A mother will forgive the mistakes and shortcomings of her child. The child also knows that no one other than the mother can protect and save him. For this reason, anyone can worship God as the Mother.

The message of Navarātri is to regard everything in the universe lovingly and reverentially. We must gain this attitude through Navarātri. This is also a time to look within silently while observing religious vows. People from all walks of life worship Śakti, the primordial power. Students place their books at the altar for worshipping; farmers and traders place their tools and implements; soldiers worship their weapons. The principle behind this pūjā is to offer our means of living to God, to seek Her blessings by worshipping Her, and to step anew into our sphere of activity with the humility and enthusiasm of a beginner.

Navarātri reminds us that time, effort and divine grace are needed to succeed in any sphere of life. For example, we won't wait until a child is 15 years old before enrolling him in kindergarten. There is a time for that. Similarly, there is a time for sowing seeds. Even if we act at the right time, our action will not bear fruit if our effort is incomplete. We might sow seeds at the right time, add sufficient fertilizer and water, and weed the area properly. But if the rainfall is untimely, the entire crop will be destroyed. In short, even if we act at the right time and put in the proper effort, we will not succeed without God's grace. Navarātri reminds us of this truth.

During Navarātri, devotees recite the *Lalitā Sahasranāma* and the *Dēvī Māhātmyam*, and observe vows according to their abilities. But such worship and other spiritual practices are not meant to be carried out only in certain seasons or on holy days. They must become an indispensable part of our daily life, like inhalation and exhalation. Likewise, there is no point in praying to a hundred gods for a hundred needs. We ought to have *tattwattile bhakti*, devotion based on an understanding of spiritual principles. We must select a form of God that we like the most as our *iṣṭa-dēvatā* (favorite form of divinity), and worship that deity alone as our own Self. We must consider all other divine forms as different manifestations of our iṣṭa-dēvatā. We ought to worship God for God alone, and not only for the sake of fulfilling our desires. Devotion should be for the sake of devotion alone. We can gain everything through devotion to God, through tattwattile bhakti. Let us worship the compassionate Jagadambā, with an awareness of the principle behind worship, for knowledge, prosperity and the ultimate goal of life, spiritual liberation.

Dīpāvali

Children, India is the land of festivals. The true purpose of a festival is to redirect the mind, which is steeped in worldly matters, to the remembrance of God. Dīpāvali is the festival of lamps. It is the festival of light. Light symbolizes goodness and knowledge. We light lamps during Dīpāvali to symbolize the kindling of knowledge within us.

Even if we light a thousand lamps from a single wick, the flame from the first wick will shine just as brightly. This reminds us that no matter how much knowledge we impart to others, our knowledge will not diminish even a little. Such is the greatness of knowledge. Similarly, the noble thoughts and good deeds of an individual also influence many others. During festivals, everyone has similar thoughts. Everyone becomes immersed in the contemplation of God. They sing devotional songs and rejoice together. The vibrations of bliss spread all around, and can bring joy and inspire thoughts of God in others also.

Amma is reminded of a story. There was a village on the outskirts of a forest. As there were no streetlights in that village, thieves began to waylay and rob travelers with increasing frequency. Occasionally, even murders were committed under the cover of darkness. When the crime rate increased, the villagers requested officials for streetlights to be installed. Despite making many requests and even meeting senior officials personally, nothing came of their efforts. There was no reduction in the crimes.

One day, a villager decided to light a lantern and keep it in front of his house, thinking that he would be able to illuminate a small area at least. At twilight, he lit a lantern and placed it in front of his house, so that the light fell on the path in front. Seeing this, his neighbor also lit a lantern and kept it in front of his house. Other neighbors began doing the same thing. Before long, every home in the village had a lantern in front, and the village became brightly lit. Robberies and murders stopped. The menace of thieves disappeared. The good deed that one man did brought about a huge transformation in the village. The changes in the mind of an individual create transformations in society.

Festivals must become opportunities to purify the human mind and awaken the goodness within. That said, we must ask ourselves if this is happening today. Often, we misuse money in the name of festivals to organize programs that pollute the human mind. This defeats the purpose of festivals.

Dīpāvali is usually associated with both Lord Kṛṣṇa and Lord Rāma. It is said that when Śrī Kṛṣṇa slayed Narakāsura, the latter prayed, "May my sorrow bring goodness to the world." We must try to cultivate a mind that prays and strives for the peace and joy of others, even when we are suffering. May the lamps we light this year for Dīpāvali inspire us to pray in this way.

Independence Day[25]

1

Children, we believe that all our problems will end if we have the freedom to look, listen and talk as we like. But this is a mistaken belief. Just as a lack of freedom causes sorrow, unbridled freedom also leads to sorrow and suffering.

Compared to the people in India, people in the West have much more external freedom. Yet, they also face sorrow and disappointment. True freedom is not external; it comes from within. We must discover it within ourselves. If we can liberate ourselves from our desires, likes and dislikes, then we will always be free, no matter what the circumstance.

Today, the West is abandoning materialism and turning towards spirituality. Westerners have started to delve into the culture of India and are accepting it, whereas we are sinking ever deeper into the pit of materialism and are in a terrible hurry to imitate the West. We swallow what they chew and spit out, considering it of great value. We ignore the values of Sanātana Dharma.

Westerners believe something only after they have studied it thoroughly. Thereafter, they will stand firm in their belief.

25 India's Independence Day, which commemorates the country's independence from British imperial rule, is celebrated on August 15th every year.

But we are just the opposite. Our faith, confined to the temple, is so fragile that it will crack as soon as someone criticizes it. Knowledge must be doubt-free and have deep roots. Such knowledge can withstand any attack. Logical thinking and inquiry must become a habit. Today, we learn about and evaluate the culture of India from books that Westerners have written. This must change.

Amma has visited many countries in the world. In every country, people respect and take pride in their traditions and customs. The indigenous people of Australia, Africa and America take pride in their traditions. But we have neither knowledge about our culture nor do we take pride in it. Many have contempt for it. Only if the foundation is deep can the structure be tall. Similarly, only if we know about our past and take pride in our heritage can we create a bright present and future.

Some may ask, "Isn't this narrow-mindedness?" Knowledge of and pride in our heritage inspire us to do good in the world. Nothing that inspires us to do good is narrow-minded. Celebrating the anniversary of India's Independence is not an occasion to blame others or ourselves but an opportunity to correct our mistakes and to become engaged in action. If everyone acts as one and with a firm resolve, we can end poverty and ignorance.

What can we do on the occasion of celebrating our independence? Those who smoke and drink can pledge to stop their bad habits. With the money saved, they can build proper homes for villagers living in huts. They can sponsor the education of children who had to stop studying because of a lack of money. The youth can clean the dirty drains in villages so that the villages become clean and free of pollution. If each one of us strives in this manner, our India will become truly prosperous. We can transform earth into heaven.

2

Children, Independence Day is here again. There cannot be anyone who doesn't desire freedom. The awareness of freedom awakens our enthusiasm and heightens our abilities. But along with an awareness of freedom, we need to cultivate a discerning intellect and a sense of responsibility.

We should think not only about our rights but also our responsibilities. All of us have a duty towards our parents, teachers and elders, society, country, culture and to all of nature. Each one of us must be ready to fulfill our duties.

No matter how great our financial gains, India, as one nation, cannot take pride in this as long as there are people starving, as long as there are illiterates in our nation, and as long as any segment of society lives in fear.

Sadly, regional, caste-based and communal politics is growing in our country. Despite the growing awareness of religion, caste and political affiliation, our awareness of social responsibilities, responsibilities to the nation, and dharmic values is decreasing. If there is a bomb blast or train accident somewhere, we won't be bothered as long as our friends or relatives are not among the victims. We might even look forward to news of the next blast. That's how selfish and self-centered we have become. That said, the bright lamps of goodness have not been completely extinguished; that is reason to hope.

When a devastating earthquake struck Gujarat, a young man's shop was completely razed. An organization involved in relief work gave him ₹100,000. When a representative from the organization asked him what he would do with this money, expecting that he would use it to rebuild his shop, the young man said, "There was a house next to my shop. A family with four children was living there. I still have a roof to sleep under. So, I shall use this money to help this family build a new home."

We need to develop such a selfless mind, one that is capable of sacrifice. We must vow to give more than we take from society. Our individual consciousness must expand into social consciousness. Awareness of our political affiliation must broaden into national awareness. Our religious identity must become a value-based one. We must expand from the feeling of 'me' to, not 'we,' but 'all of us.'

3

Children, India is celebrating her 70th Independence Day. When we look back on the trials and tribulations of the past, there is much we can be proud of. Yet, there are many problems that need to be resolved. A large number of Indians are poor and illiterate. Values have eroded. Communalism still exists.

The solution is to awaken self-confidence and the capacity for and habit of hard work in everyone. To do so, we must first gain knowledge of our culture and heritage, and be proud of them. India is the land of the *ṛṣis* (seers), who bequeathed knowledge and a culture of goodness and auspiciousness to the whole world. Exalted spiritual principles and noble values are the hallmarks of our civilization and culture. It teaches us to see and worship God in all beings, moving and unmoving, and thus to love and serve them.

We might have different customs, beliefs and outlooks. But in spite of these differences, we ought to coexist harmoniously by awakening within us an awareness of the country as a unified whole. The basis for this unity is our nation's culture.

Amma is reminded of an incident that happened centuries ago. Refugees fleeing atrocities against them in their homeland reached the shores of an Indian kingdom. The king received them, placed before them a silver pot brimming with milk, and, handing it to them, asked, "This is the symbol of our land. Tell me: how can we absorb you into this?"

The leader of the refugees took a spoonful of sugar and mixed it in the milk, where the sugar dissolved instantly. The message that this gesture conveyed was this: We will not create any unrest in the country giving us refuge. We will add joy and sweetness to the lives of her citizens. The king, who understood the message, gave the refugees the land and wealth needed to settle down comfortably in his kingdom.

Just as the footprints of every other animal can be contained within those of an elephant, India's culture is expansive and broadminded enough to accommodate different beliefs and viewpoints. If we can awaken this knowledge of and pride in our heritage, we can prevail over all sectarian and communalist sentiments, over poverty, and over the erosion of values. At the same time, we will be able to accept the good from any source, and reject the evil, wherever we find it.

Our culture and the land we are born in is our mother. If we become disconnected from our culture, we will become like kites with severed strings. If we assimilate our culture and live accordingly, we will see the dawn of peace and prosperity in both our country and the world.

4

Children, humanity has always cherished freedom since time immemorial. Freedom is as dear to each being as life itself. Freedom is absolutely necessary for the growth and development of our body, mind and intellect. But we must understand one thing: If someone misuses his freedom, he will become the cause of sorrow in the lives of many others. Their freedom will be curtailed as a result. Later, that misuse will become the cause of his own sorrow. If we understand this, we will be able to regulate our conduct.

Amma is reminded of a story. A young man used to travel by bike to meet his lover every day. In his eagerness to meet his lover, he did not obey traffic rules. He never stopped at any red traffic light. This led to frequent accidents, but that did not bother him. One day, he stopped at a red light, took out from his pocket a photo of his lover, and gazed at it until the light turned green. A friend, who was with him that day, realized that he had for once stopped at a red light. He asked, "What happened? You never used to wait so patiently at a red light."

He answered, "I used to forget everything in my eagerness to see my girlfriend. I never used to bother about traffic rules or about other vehicles. I was prompted only by the selfish goal of seeing her. But then I started thinking, 'If I meet with an accident, my girlfriend will become distressed.' So, I started paying attention to traffic rules."

Similarly, when we focus only on our own likes and dislikes, we will feel that rules and regulations are unnecessary. But when we become patient and considerate towards others, we will be ready to accept rules and regulations. There should be harmony and balance between the rights of the individual and the welfare of society. This is what the people of India call dharma. Our freedom must be rooted in dharma. This is the way to progress.

In truth, absolute freedom is not possible in life. Joy and sorrow, freedom and restriction are two sides of the coin of life. The dualities will never go away. The world has seen many billionaires and great kings who conquered many countries. In spite of this, most of them only had sorrow, disappointment and a lack of freedom by the end of their lives.

The realm of absolute freedom remains untouched by any of the sorrows and miseries of the world. This is the true state of our being, our true self, our *ātma-swarūpa*. Once we understand this, we will be able to enjoy pure and total freedom even in the midst of troubles. But an individual's spiritual progress cannot bring about the progress of a nation as a whole. That is why our ancestors gave utmost importance to progress that was firmly rooted in dharma.

The brave men and women who fought for our independence lived lives deeply rooted in dharma. If we are not aware of and do not adhere to dharma in our lives, our country will not even make material progress. On this occasion, when we celebrate yet another Independence Day, let us all take note of and become aware of this truth.

Christmas

1

Children, Christmas awakens the optimistic expectations of hope and compassion in human hearts. It reminds us that, instead of hostility and selfishness, love for God and compassion towards fellow beings ought to fill our hearts. This is what Christ showed us through his life.

Christmas is also an occasion to strengthen bonds. We might feel dislike or resentment towards our relatives, friends or colleagues if they don't live up to our expectations. Apart from misplaced expectations, we also have misconceptions about them. A thief considers everyone else to be a thief. This is because each one of us evaluates others based on our own nature and experiences.

Once, when a woman returned home from work, she saw her seven-year-old daughter standing with an apple in each of her hands. The mother lovingly asked her, "Darling daughter, would you please give mummy one of the apples?" The child glanced at her mother for a moment and then bit into the apple in her right hand. And then she bit into the apple in her left hand. Seeing this, the mother's face clouded over, but she tried to hide her disappointment. The next moment, the child lovingly offered her mother the apple in her right hand, saying, "Mummy, this is sweeter!" Though only for a moment, even her own mother could not perceive her daughter's innocent love. This story reminds us of how easy it is to misjudge others.

We might have knowledge and experience, but we must take care not to judge and blame others hastily. Our hearts must become generous enough to listen to and understand another person's point of view. We must give even those who have committed an appalling crime an opportunity to explain themselves. Our assumptions about them might be wrong.

When we give and receive gifts for Christmas, we become happy. But true gifts cannot be bought. The truest gift we can give ourselves is a new and better outlook on life. Giving up our bad habits will be the most invaluable gift we can give our loved ones, one that will make them happy. It is through such good transformations that Christmas can truly illumine our lives.

2

Children, Christmas has come to spread the message of devotion to God and love for humanity. Christmas awakens the feelings of compassion and goodness in human hearts. It reminds us that instead of hatred and selfishness, love for God and compassion for our fellow beings ought to fill our hearts.

There is a spiritual principle behind the birth of Christ. He was not born in a palace but in a manger. His parents were neither rich nor were they great scholars. They had nothing to call their own, other than their pure hearts. Not many people knew of Christ's nativity, except a few blessed ones. The message that this conveys is that only seekers who are humble and patient will experience a spiritual awakening. "Remove the ego from your heart. I shall dwell therein." This is God's message.

Christ's humble birth heralded the compassion and humility that was seen throughout his life. He lived not as a king but as one among the people, always ready to serve. As such, he was always accessible to the suffering and downtrodden. However lofty our position in life, we must be broadminded enough to see everyone equally. We can see this quality in Christ.

Through the story of the Good Samaritan, Christ teaches that a man becomes noble not by power and position but by the goodness and love within his heart. Love for God and love for humanity are not two different things but two sides of the same coin. Love is God. If we get an opportunity to help the sorrowful and the downtrodden, we must seize it. The teachings of Christ, like India's spiritual philosophy, makes this clear.

The core message of Christmas is to love and share. We must become aware of the pain of others less fortunate than we are. They may not have enough money to celebrate Christmas. Such occasions are an opportunity for us to honor Christ's teaching: "Love thy neighbor as thyself."

It is not enough to think only of ourselves. We must look around and understand the needs of others. If we can help at least one person, it will spread the light of goodness in that person's life. If each one of us can help someone, that would be a true celebration of Christmas. May Christmas inspire my children to soar into the skies of peace and happiness.

Criticism

Children, usually, we don't like other people criticizing or finding fault with us. Many of us become uncomfortable when we hear criticism. Some become sad while others protest. Yet others launch a counter attack. Anyone will justify his or her own viewpoint eagerly. But this is not how we ought to respond to criticisms and allegations. If we welcome criticism with alertness and a positive mindset, we can use it to catalyze our growth and enlarge our vision.

Anonymous articles severely criticizing the ruler of a country used to appear regularly in an underground newspaper. Secret agents uncovered the identity of the journalist and brought him before the ruler. Everyone became anxious over the fate of the journalist. But the ruler told the journalist, "I have read your articles. You have analyzed my actions and motivations in detail. Often, I understood my mistakes only from your articles. If you become my secretary, I will be able to rectify my mistakes and rule the country much better." The journalist accepted the offer and became his secretary.

It is usually difficult for us to understand our own mistakes and shortcomings. Even if we do understand them, we are likely to regard them as trivial and thus dismiss them. But people are generally highly skilled at spotting the mistakes and shortcomings of others. For this very reason, we ought to receive the criticisms directed at us, with utmost attentiveness. They will often be baseless. But if we examine them carefully, we can learn about our shortcomings. This will help us to correct our mistakes and grow. Therefore, we must always feel gratitude towards our critics.

A rose is undoubtedly beautiful. But what about the fertilizer given to the rose bush? We use cow dung and tea leaves. Such manure is needed for beautiful flowers to bud and blossom. Similarly, we need the compost of criticism and opposition for our spiritual growth.

Even if the criticism is baseless, our response ought to be moderate, calm and collected. We must not even think about taking revenge on those who criticize us. Instead, we must pray, "O God! Make them good. Bless them with a kind heart!"

We must cultivate the ability to receive criticism calmly. If we succeed in doing so, we will experience peace and calm, be able to rectify our mistakes, and thus grow.

Awakening the Inner Strength

Children, many of us fail in life because we do not recognize our own abilities and do not know how to utilize them properly. Whatever the field of activity, understanding our own strengths and weaknesses is crucial to our success. The truth is that there is limitless strength and potential lying dormant in everyone. If we nurture these qualities, we can overcome any crisis in life successfully.

Once, while a man was driving a truck along the highway, the truck caught fire. The man stopped the truck, went to a phone booth nearby, and called the fire brigade, which came quickly and put out the fire. When the fire fighters opened the back door of the truck, they saw that half of it was full of furniture. Unfortunately, it had been gutted by the fire. When they examined the other half of the truck, they were astonished. It was full of fire extinguishers! But the driver was unaware of this. If he had known, he could have extinguished the fire immediately. Our situation is like that of the driver in the story. All too often, we remain ignorant of our abilities or utilise only a fraction of them.

Suppose a company bought a supercomputer worth millions of rupees and used it only for its accounts. What a colossal waste! An ordinary computer would have sufficed for that purpose. The company is not using even one percent of the supercomputer's capacity. Similarly, we, too, underutilize our lives. Let's take another example. A porter uses his head to carry heavy loads whereas a scientist uses his head to unveil the secrets of nature. The latter's discoveries benefit all of humanity. Everyone has a head and a brain. But only a rare few harness the brain's full potential.

If you place a heavy burden on the shoulders of a man who is not used to carrying heavy weights, he will collapse. But if he puts his mind to it, he can enhance his physical strength through persistent effort and gradually increase the weight that he can carry. Finally, he will be able to lift even huge weights effortlessly. Similarly, through unceasing effort, we can bring out and enhance our hidden talents and achieve great ends.

Determination

Children, there are two kinds of people: those who act without thinking, and those who think without acting. The first kind either acts without thinking or thinks wrongly and gets into trouble. Their actions benefit neither them nor others; not only that, they also cause harm. The second kind reflects duly on a matter and can distinguish right from wrong, but they do not follow up with action. They may advise others, but going around preaching is akin to trying to heal oneself of disease by asking others to take medication.

We make plans to do many noble deeds. But we also think of ways and means to avoid doing them. There was an ancient temple where devotees used to come once a week to chant and pray while fasting. A monkey watching them thought, "They fast and pray and thus gain blessings from God. Why can't I do the same thing?" The very next fasting day, the monkey sat under a tree within the temple precincts. As soon as it started meditating, a thought arose: "I've never fasted before for even a day in my entire life. What if, by the time the fast ends today, I'm too tired even to get up and walk? I'll collapse and die in this spot itself! If I sit under a fruit tree, I won't have to go anywhere in search of food."

Thinking thus, the monkey got up, went to a tree laden with many fruits, sat under it, and started meditating. After a while, it thought, "If I become too weak to climb up the tree after the fast, that will be the end of me!" This led the monkey to climb to a branch laden with fruit. It then started meditating. Soon, it thought, "What if my arms lack the strength to pluck the fruits when the fast ends?" The monkey plucked all the fruits it needed, kept them in its lap, and started meditating. After a while, it became hungry. He thought, "I've not had such big and sweet fruits in a long time. I can always fast on another day!" And before the monkey knew it, the fruits in its lap had already reached its mouth!

Many of us are like the monkey in this story. Our mind will continue finding excuses to avoid doing what is necessary. Along with knowledge, we must have determination and an awareness of the goal. Those who are determined to complete the tasks they have resolved to do, no matter what the obstacle, will definitely succeed in life.

Contradictions

Children, one could well say that contradiction is the hallmark of human life. One can see contradictions everywhere.

We dedicate expensive garlands and wreaths to the deceased but are not willing to give them even one flower when they are alive. We compose odes to glorify the deceased but malign them when they are alive.

We buy life insurance because we know that death can come at any moment. Yet most of us act as if death can never claim us. We rush frantically after name and fame, and toil to accumulate mountains of wealth.

Today, we have made our homes, offices and shops secure. We don't allow any troublemaker inside. But we have kept wide open all the doors of our mind for troublemakers. As a result, these troublemakers enter our mind whenever they please and steal all that is precious. These troublemakers are our bad thoughts. They steal the wealth of peace.

We are interested in solving our financial problems, but in our frenzy are not aware of an increasing deficit in our lives: the dearth of true happiness. In our rush for all things material, we lose true happiness.

Today, our heads are hot and our hearts are cold. The heat of the head is from the ego, and the coldness of the heart, from selfishness. It ought to be the other way around. The heart ought to be warm with love and compassion. At the same time, the head ought to be cool with the broadmindedness of true knowledge. If the mind is calm and peaceful, the head will be cool. Our thoughts will be clear and bright.

Why is our life full of contradictions? It is because our thoughts, words and deeds are not in harmony with our conscience. All four should move together in tandem. If they are not aligned, the mind will be riddled with conflict. Life will become agitated by contradictions. Conversely, if the four coexist harmoniously, peace and happiness will blossom in the mind. The body will become healthy. The river of life will flow seamlessly. For this to happen, we must live with awareness.

We must be ready to assimilate values without hesitation. It is high time that humanity awoke from the darkness of selfishness and lovelessness into the bright light of compassion and acceptance. The present moment is for us to understand our responsibilities to the world and to ourselves.

Rebirth

Children, some people ask if there is such a thing as rebirth. A mother can give birth to twins, one of whom is handicapped, and the other, perfectly healthy. One person leads a sorrowful life whereas another person lives joyfully. How can we explain such discrepancies? The only explanation we can give is that each is experiencing the consequences of actions done in past lives.

Karma (action) is the cause of life. The purpose of each birth is to experience the fruits of actions done in previous lives. Just as it is difficult to say if the seed or fruit came first, it is hard to say if birth or karma came first.

If we lead good lives doing noble deeds, we will receive higher births. But if we live like animals even after obtaining human births, we will be reborn in inferior wombs. This cycle of birth and death will continue until we gain knowledge of the Self and attain spiritual liberation.

Some people ask why they don't remember the actions done in past lives if they have been born before. We don't remember many of the events from this life even! We might forget the song that we memorized yesterday. Likewise, we have forgotten what happened in our previous lives. But if our mind becomes subtle enough through meditation, we will be able to recollect everything.

Our next life depends on our thoughts at the time of death. For example, if, at the time of death, a man thinks of his partially built house, he will be reborn to fulfill the desire to finish building the house.

There once lived a wealthy man who was extremely intelligent. He named all his children after gods. He thought that if he called out to his children at the time of death, like Ajāmila[26] had done, he would die uttering the names of the Lord, and thus attain spiritual liberation without any further effort. When death drew near, he called all his children: "Rāmā! Gōvindā! Nārāyaṇā!" All his sons gathered around him. The rich man looked at them and then angrily asked, "If all of you come here, who will take care of the shop?" As soon as he said this, he died. Our habits and tendencies determine our final thoughts.

There is no need to worry about what will happen after death. What is important is our present life and the present moment. If we do good deeds and live wisely in each moment, we can live contentedly, both now and in the future. When we realize that we are not the perishable body but the embodiment of *sat-cit-ānanda* (truth-consciousness-bliss), we will transcend birth and death and experience eternal peace.

26 Character in the Bhāgavata Purāṇa. His life illustrates the point that there is hope for redemption for even the sinful, if they chant God's name.

The Sense of Being a Doer

Children, at present, our every thought, word and deed are imbued with the sense of "I'm doing it." As long as we have this attitude, we will not receive God's grace, no matter how much we work. Therefore, let us give up the 'I' sense and cultivate instead the feeling that we are working with God-given strength. Let us also nurture the attitude of dedicating all that we do to Him.

While driving at night, we can see along the highway many reflective signs showing the way. They are quite bright. Suppose the board thinks, "It's only because of me that the vehicles know which way to go!" Actually, the signs are luminous only because the headlights from vehicles fall on them. The boards are not self-effulgent. Similarly, we all say, "I'm doing this." We don't think about where we got the strength to do the work. We become arrogant, like the signboards along the highway. We forget that without the animating power from God, we won't be able to move even our little finger.

Our hands might lose the ability to move even while we say, "I'm doing everything!" What will we do then? How many seconds does it take for our breath to stop? Who knows for sure when we will stop breathing? Similarly, we have no control over the fruits of our actions. Many factors must come together before any act can give its intended result. These factors will come together only if we have God's grace. In short, it is by divine power alone that everything happens in this world. This does not mean that we need not put in any effort but that we must act with the attitude that we are merely instruments in His hands.

A child bought her mother a birthday present. She went to her mother and said, "Look mum, I've got you a nice gift!" and offered it to her mother.

Looking at the gift, the mother asked her, "Where did you get the money to buy the gift?"

The daughter said, "I used the pocket money you gave me."

Similarly, we say, "I'm doing this!" In truth, God gave us the strength to say those words and to do the work. We must not forget this. We must try to cultivate the attitude that we are only instruments in God's hands. Then, divine grace will naturally flow into and fill our hearts.

Heaven and Hell

Children, people today are frenetically rushing here and there for a drop of peace. We toil to make the outer world a heaven but don't realize that our inner world has become like hell. In today's world, there is no dearth of luxury items. There are more air-conditioned rooms and cars than are needed, and yet, we lack peace of mind. Many people lie down inside these air-conditioned rooms, but need to take sleeping pills to get some sleep. Unable to bear the mental conflict, many people commit suicide. If peace and happiness could be found in external objects, then a life of luxury would give us peace and happiness. But that is not what we see. If only those who were so impatient to air-condition their cars and rooms had learnt to air-condition their minds first! That is the only way to real happiness. Spiritual knowledge teaches us to air-condition the mind. It is the science of the mind. That is true knowledge.

Once, a new visitor to an āśram asked the Guru, "Do heaven and hell really exist?"

The Guru asked him, "Who are you?"

"I'm a warrior," said the man proudly.

Hearing this, the Guru said, "You are cruel and animal-like! What right does someone like you have to ask this question? Don't waste my time. Leave!"

The warrior could not bear this affront. He unsheathed his sword and angrily lunged at the Guru to kill him. At that moment, the Guru said, "Your mind is filled with anger. You are now in hell."

When he heard this, the warrior was filled with contrition. His anger melted before the wisdom of the Guru. He slid his sword into the scabbard and humbly bowed down to the Guru. The Guru said, "You are now in heaven."

Heaven and hell are our own creations. If the mind is at peace, even the worst hell will become heaven. If the mind is unsettled, even the most exalted heaven will feel like hell. Peace, contentment and happiness are dependent on one's mind and not on external objects or situations. Therefore, we must learn to control the mind. One who knows this grieves no more. He or she will experience only unending bliss.

Unending or eternal bliss is *mōkṣa* (spiritual liberation). It transcends heaven and hell. One can experience it even while on earth. Those who realize, "I am not the body, which is subject to birth and death, but the imperishable Self" are always in bliss. They see God in everything and do only good. They are truly brave and do not fear even death. Nothing affects them.

Humility

Children, humility is an invaluable virtue and the royal path to progress. Humility destroys the ego and ushers in goodness. Knowledge and grace flow only to the humble. No matter how heavily rain falls on a mountaintop, the water will not stay there. But if there is a hole in the ground, it will fill up with water.

Bowing down to others is not a weakness. If a man going to bathe in the river says, "I won't bow my head to the river. I will not dip into the water," he will not be able to cleanse his body. When we say that we will not bow down before anyone, the only thing that will remain intact is our ignorance. That said, humility without discernment is also not of much use. It is a mere show.

Once, a king went to a temple to pray. As it was still early in the morning, there was no one else there. The king started praying, "O God, I am no one. I am only a speck of dust on your feet." As soon as he said this, the king heard someone else praying. Turning around, he saw someone praying a short distance away. He was using the very same words the king had uttered. The king felt resentful. He asked loudly, "Who just said 'I am no one'? When I have said 'I am no one,' who else dares to make the same claim?" The king walked towards the devotee to see who he was. He was a beggar. The king said, "When the king of this country says, I am no one,' no one else has the right to say it, especially a beggar like you! You are not fit to utter those words." The feeling that we are humble is often just our fancy. If so, 'humility' is just a mask for our arrogance and ignorance. Hence, we must always be alert.

If we wish to receive God's grace, there must be humility in our words and actions. Towering trees and buildings can come crashing down under the onslaught of a fierce hurricane, but even the strongest gale can do nothing to a blade of grass. This is the greatness of humility.

Even if we have every other noble virtue but not humility, we will not excel in any field. We will not be able to please others or make them happy. The chances of failing are very high. But if we have humility, everyone will like us and be happy with us even if we have many shortcomings. We will succeed easily.

It is not enough to study the scriptures. We must have the attitude of bowing down to everything. At present, we are filled with the 'I' sense. While they are unripe, the cluster of coconuts will stand tall. But when they ripen, the cluster will bend down. When knowledge matures, humility dawns naturally. Humility makes one as expansive as the universe. That is why it is said, "If you become a zero, you become a hero!" Humility awakens the real greatness in us and makes us one with the infinite divine consciousness.

Cultivate Good Habits

Children, there is increasing corruption, erosion of values, and assaults against women in society. What is the reason for this? The world today is like a supermarket. Everything is on open display. Many things tempt us. The influence of the Internet, mobile phones and other media is pervasive. Under these circumstances, we need to have a strong sense of values and be firmly rooted in dharma if we wish to bring about harmony and stability. Those values and foundation in dharma must be given to children from a young age.

It is not enough to scold or punish them. Young minds must be guided to goodness. We must set good examples and encourage them when they do good. They must not be chained only to studies. We must give them enough freedom to nourish their imagination, intellect and emotions. At the same time, we must also point out what is right and what is wrong, what is dharmic and what is adharmic. Encouragement and intelligent intervention can accomplish what scolding or advising may not.

Amma recalls an incident. A child was in the habit of regularly wasting a lot of food. His father lovingly tried explaining to him why he must not waste food. When that did not work, the father scolded him sternly. That did not work either. He wanted to change his son's bad habit somehow. One day, the father showed him a video. The first scene showed two girls sitting in a restaurant and eating chicken. For some time, they were joking and laughing. They stopped eating and threw the rest of the food into the waste bin.

After a while, a poor man came and started rummaging through the waste bin. When he saw two large pieces of chicken, his face lit up with happiness. He kept the two pieces inside a small plastic bag. He collected the rest of the food in the waste bin and went home with it. His children ran up to him and started opening up the plastic bags one by one. They eagerly took out the left over *dōsa* (Indian pancake) and pieces of bread from the packets and started devouring them. The man then took out the two pieces of chicken from the plastic bag that he had kept aside and gave them to his children. Their faces blossomed in joy. In no time, they made short work of the food. Still hungry, they started licking the plastic bags.

By the time he finished watching the video, the boy's eyes had welled up with tears. He said, "Dad, I'll never ever waste food again!"

Imparting values at a young age is very important. We can make imprints on cement before it dries, but once it is set, it is impossible. Hence, alongside love and affection, parents must also impart values and good advice to their children. Parents must try to become role models for their children. Then, children will gradually acquire a dharmic consciousness and good habits. They will be able to resist temptations. Children must learn that the goal of life is not just to earn money and enjoy themselves; they must realize that there is something greater. Once they gain this understanding, society will gradually become more virtuous and there will be progress in all spheres of life.

Conquer the Mind

Children, the mind is a good servant but a bad master. We mustn't allow the mind to master us. The more attached the mind is to worldly objects, the less control we will have over it. Before long, the mind will become our master.

A boy went to a school that gave children lessons in horseback riding. For some time, he carefully watched as the trainers helped the other children mount the horses and ride them. When the trainers went for lunch, he quietly mounted a horse, which started galloping wildly. Seeing this, the boy's friend shouted, "Where are you off to?"

The boy said, "I have no idea! Ask the horse!"

This is also how things are with us. Like the horse in this story, our mind is taking us for a wild ride. Only the horse of our mind knows where it is going. The truth is that we don't have the slightest control over the mind.

At present, we are in the grip of the mind. This must change. We must get a grip on the mind and make it an instrument in our hands. Right now, the mind is using us. In short, the mind is the master and we are its servant. This is the main reason for all our problems.

It is difficult to gain control of ourselves if we are addicted to something, if we are too near it. A habitual drinker resolved to stop drinking from the next day. He made this decision when the bottle of alcohol was kept next to his pillow. When he woke up the next morning, his first thought was, "Should I drink or not?" While pondering over this, his hands automatically reached for the bottle. Our habits form our character, which controls us.

Someone who wishes to bring the mind under control must initially stay away from situations that tempt him, and then strive to control his mind. Those who are learning to drive first practice on an open ground. Once they have learnt to drive, they can drive even on the highway. Similarly, if we train the mind for a while in solitude, we will be able to control it to a large extent in any situation. Victory over the mind is true victory and true liberty.

Dharma and Adharma

Children, dharma is what sustains the harmony and rhythm of the universe. Everyone desires and strives for comfort and joy. While seeking comfort and joy, let us not forget that others also desire the same things. When we receive anything from society, we also have a responsibility to give something back in return. If we are not prepared to do so, the harmony and rhythm of society will be disturbed. But if we give more than we take, peace and unity will prevail, and dharma will flourish.

It is not wrong at all to take what we reasonably need from nature. But taking more than we need and taking unlawfully is unrighteous. For example, using four buckets of water to bathe when we need only one is unrighteous. Our wrongdoing might be the cause of another person not even getting enough water to drink. When we waste food, we are responsible for denying food to a starving man.

Excessive luxury is unrighteous and sinful. Hence, we must always avoid ostentation and extravagance. But that's not enough. We must also use the money we save to help the poor and needy. The purpose of avoiding overspending is not to hoard money like misers. If each person does his or her part to help society, society will in turn take care of his or her needs. This is what the saying 'dharma protects those who protect it' means.

Once, a rich and selfish man submitted a complaint to the village judge. He accused the defendant of stealing money from his cupboard. The defendant admitted to the crime. The judge delivered an unusual sentence. He sentenced both plaintiff and defendant to imprisonment. When the king heard about this, he summoned the judge and asked him, "Was it right to impose the same sentence on both of them? Why did you send the rich man to jail? What was his crime?"

The judge said, "His crime was that he amassed more wealth than he needed. Not only did he not spend it on righteous causes, he did not donate it to those who are capable of doing good to society. Though God gave him eyes, he turned a blind eye to those around him who are suffering without food, clothing and shelter. That is his crime."

The judge paused for a while and then said, "I think that it wasn't right of me to impose the same sentence on both of them. The rich man ought to be punished also for abetting the thief to do wrong. If the rich man had used his wealth properly to help the needy, he would not have created a thief in society."

The mistakes we make because of carelessness are just as unrighteous as extravagance. For example, if a store owner does not properly count his money and secure it, he will tempt workers to steal. Thus, he will also be complicit in abetting his workers to commit a crime.

Dharma is doing the right action at the right time in the right manner. To a large extent, it is our selfishness and carelessness that tempts others to do wrong. Only if every person exercises restraint can everyone lead a comfortable and secure life.

Extravagance and Luxury

Children, in recent times, there have been significant changes in social attitudes. Until two generations ago, simple living and sacrifice were considered the ideals of a noble life. But today, most people give importance to material comforts. Extravagance and luxury have become a way of life.

There are people who spend tens of thousands of rupees on comforts and luxuries. At the same time, the next-door neighbor might be starving for want of money to buy food. A family is not able to conduct the daughter's marriage because it cannot afford a dowry of a thousand rupees. Elsewhere, the husband's family sends the wife back to her parents' home because the dowry seems inadequate to them. At the same time, some families spend millions to celebrate their daughter's wedding extravagantly. There are countless such examples.

In India, weddings are often extravagant. A marriage could be conducted in the registrar's office. But a marriage is an auspicious event, an occasion for family and friends to gather. In the old days, marriage rituals were regarded primarily as an occasion for the bride and groom to please relatives, friends and neighbors, to seek their blessings, and to infuse the sweetness of peace and happiness into the lives of the newly-weds. But times are changing. We should not give too much importance to external decorations. If we have even a little compassion, we will reduce unnecessary expenditure and use the money saved to sponsor the marriage of poor girls.

Another noteworthy phenomenon is our craze for gold. People in general and Malayāḷīs in particular have become socially conditioned to perceive gold as a synonym for girl. Brides are adorned with more gold than a caparison covering an elephant. If gold does not cover the neck and arms, people feel an incompleteness. Excessive gold is like a badge of pride. Amma does not think that it is wrong to buy gold. Doing so wisely is an investment. But an obsession with gold is unwise. It is dangerous for parents to take loans and mortgage their property to buy gold for their children. Actually, many girls today are not particularly crazy about gold. The importance given to gold is socially cultivated.

We must practice moderation and simplicity in all things. We can take what we need. But taking more than what we need is adharmic. If we need only five sets of clothes, it is excessive and unrighteous to have ten. Consuming natural resources rapaciously without thinking about the needs of others is a crime against humanity. We must take care not to waste water while washing plates and our hands and while bathing. If we see the lights and fans switched on in a room but no one is there, we must turn them off. We must be especially careful about food. What right do we have to waste food when millions in the world are starving?

If we can find happiness in the wellbeing of others instead of our own selfish interests, our life will be blessed. If we are prepared to spend the money we squander on bad habits and luxuries, to help the suffering and those who cannot afford even one meal a day, we can spread the light of goodness in both their lives and ours.

Food and the Mind

Children, we take care to eat nutritious food so that we can safeguard the health of our body. The food we eat influences not just the body but our mind and thoughts as well. The subtle part of food becomes the mind. Purity of food leads to purity of mind. Eating certain kinds of food can cause negative emotions. Therefore, those who do spiritual practices must be careful about what they eat.

It is not possible to control the mind without controlling what we eat. We ought to eat to sustain the health of body and mind, and not to satiate our taste buds. Unless we give up the taste of the tongue, we won't gain the taste of the heart.

The thought vibrations of those who prepare the food will be transmitted to those who eat the food. A *sannyāsī* (monk) who never read newspapers started dreaming about news. He wondered why. One day, he saw the āśram cook reading the newspaper while cooking food. Then he understood why he was having those dreams. While the cook was reading the newspaper, sometimes the fire would start to go out. Without taking his eyes away from the newspaper, he would stoke the fire. All his attention was on the newspaper. The thoughts he had while cooking influenced the ascetic. Therefore, as far as possible, mothers should take it upon themselves to cook food for the family. If the food is prepared while chanting the mantra, then the food becomes sanctified and will benefit everyone in the family.

Before eating, we ought to feed our pets first or give some food to birds and other animals. Offer this food as *nivēdya* (food offered to God), while imagining your *iṣṭa-dēvatā* (favorite form of divinity) in these creatures.

When we sit down to eat, we should first set aside one morsel as an offering to our iṣṭa-dēvatā. Then, we can close our eyes for two minutes and pray, "O God, may this food give me the strength to see and serve You in everyone. May it lead me to Self-realization." While eating, we must concentrate not only on the taste but also imagine that we are feeding our iṣṭa-dēvatā within us. That way, even eating becomes a form of worship.

We must not eat until our stomach is full. Half the stomach should be for food, and a quarter for water. We must leave a quarter for air to circulate. This will aid in digestion. If we eat until we can barely breathe, the heart will have to bear a heavier workload. This is bad for our health. Eating at regular times is good for health; it also helps us gain control over the mind. We must eat to live and not live to eat.

Facing Change

Children, change is the nature of life. Not being able to face changes in the right manner is the root cause of all our problems.

Change plays a vital role in the growth and progress of humanity. Enthusiasm, excitement and creativity are meaningful only in an ever-changing world. Action becomes relevant only then. It is change that develops our mind, body and strength. If there were no change, this world would be filled with lazy and dim-witted people.

Yet, behind all change lies a changeless substratum. Understanding this is our real goal. But today, many live forgetting this goal. We are like the traveler who boards a bus, starts daydreaming, and forgets to alight at his stop. We are frantically seeking something or the other for some dream world. We have forgotten that our real goal is peace.

There was a farmer who would forget many things while caught up in his work. He started drawing multicolored lines on a piece of paper to remind himself of the most important tasks that needed to be done the next day. Each line represented a specific task. One night, he drew seven lines to remind him of seven tasks that had to be completed the next day. They were like the seven colors of the rainbow. When he woke up, he drew another line. Now, there were eight lines. The first line was for his daily routine: brushing his teeth, bathing and so on. The second was to take his dog for a walk. The third was to water and add fertilizer to his crop. The fourth was to buy things from the market. The fifth was to feed the cows. The sixth was to repair the car. And the seventh was to pay the electricity bill. After completing these tasks, he wondered, "What's the eighth line for?" Night fell and he still couldn't remember. He tried hard to recall. He walked up and down and became so stressed that he could not sleep. Finally, at dawn, he recalled what the eighth line meant: to sleep well. The doctor had specifically advised him to go to bed early every night.

This is how we forget our goal. The aim of human life is to reach God. This is the unchanging goal. But we are striving to change some things and to stop some other things from changing. Because of this, we are constantly stressed. But if our attention were firmly fixed on God, the unchanging goal, then no change will affect us. We will welcome every change. Life will become filled with contentment.

Keep Up the Enthusiasm

Children, all of us endeavor to achieve many things but we do not always succeed in our efforts. What is the foundation of success? It is enthusiasm, effort and optimistic faith. We must keep up our enthusiasm even if we come up against unfavorable circumstances or make mistakes.

If we fall, we must pick ourselves up and forge ahead enthusiastically. We must see the fall as a warning to be more attentive and not to fall again. There is no point in brooding over it. What use is there in crying over a wound? Instead of crying, we must apply medicine to it. If we fall down while walking, we won't remain lying on the ground. We will get up and continue walking. Similarly, even if we face a setback, we must continue to strive without giving undue importance to the fall.

It may be that we do not see any appreciable result for all our efforts. We might feel that there is no cause for hope. Nevertheless, we must continue striving with confidence. Faith and effort will never be futile.

Once, a few goat kids were grazing on a mountain slope. When they saw a vineyard of grapes at the top of the mountain, the kids became excited and wanted to get there. They started trotting up the mountain. Seeing this, the adult goats said, "Hey, where are you going? The vineyard is too high! You can't climb so high. You're already starting to drag your feet. Come down, kids! You can't pull off this feat." Hearing this, the enthusiasm of the goat kids started waning, and one by one, they turned around. A few continued to rush forward. The adult goats shouted, "Come down! Come down! You cannot climb the mountain." Hearing this, the rest of the kids turned around and started coming down. One kid alone continued trotting up and finally reached the vineyard. It ate the grapes to its heart's content. When it returned, all its friends applauded enthusiastically and warmly welcomed the goat kid.

A man who was watching all this asked, "So many goat kids attempted to scale the mountain, but you alone had the strength and stamina needed to reach the summit. Why?"

The kid did not say anything. The man asked again, "Please tell me. Your feat was marvelous! How could a kid like you pull off this feat?"

The kid's mother answered, "My son is deaf."

Children, there will be many situations that destroy our faith and dampen our enthusiasm. There will be problems and obstacles. We might hear discouraging words. We must turn a deaf ear to them and head towards the goal courageously and without flagging, like that goat kid. If we can do that, we will definitely succeed.

Some people accomplish things that others consider impossible. How is that possible? It is possible through unshakeable determination and tireless enthusiasm. When our resolve is firm, our inner strength awakens. It can achieve wondrous things. Children, strive with faith and firm commitment, and you will certainly accomplish great things.

Coexistence

Children, one feature that is present everywhere in the universe is infinite diversity. Diversity is the hallmark of creation. Generally, all creatures accept diversity and coexist peacefully. Man alone does not. He fights and kills in the name of nation, language, religion, race, caste and the like. The cause of this is a mind filled with fear, doubt and hatred of those who are different from him.

Three men set out on a long pilgrimage. They crossed rivers and hills and finally came to the base of a huge mountain. There, a monk joined them. Even though the pilgrims did not like the monk, who was from another country and who dressed differently, they tried not to express their dislike outwardly. But from that day onwards, their journey started becoming more and more difficult. They struggled because of heavy rains, thunder and lightning. As they were traveling through uninhabited terrain, they could not get food and drinking water. The three pilgrims suspected that the monk was the cause of all their hardship.

One day, there was a heavy downpour, and the travelers took shelter in a ramshackle hut. One of the pilgrims said, "One among us is unlucky and sinful. God is angry with him. That's why all of us are suffering so much. Let's do this: Each one of us must step out of the hut and stand in the open. God will punish the one who has incurred His wrath. The others can then resume their pilgrimage at ease."

Accordingly, all of them took turns to stand in the open. Nothing happened to the three pilgrims. Finally, the monk stepped out of the hut. As soon as he did, there was a resounding clap of thunder, and lightning struck the hut, reducing it to ash in seconds. In truth, it was the spiritual merit of the monk that had been protecting the other three all along.

We ought not to disrespect or vilify those who are different from us. Instead, we must awaken and nourish the awareness that we are all children of one God and fundamentally equal, and thus rise above our differences.

It is only when seven different hues come together that a beautiful rainbow is formed. Similarly, the world becomes beautiful when different countries, religions, languages and cultures come together. We must accept this principle and accord primary importance to humaneness and the human race, and with mutual cooperation, move forward as one.

Mōkṣa

The scriptures say that the highest goal of human life is *mōkṣa* (spiritual liberation). It is the attainment of supreme bliss. It is neither the experience of heaven and hell nor elevation into the abode of one's favorite deity after death but total freedom from all kinds of attachment and sorrow.

Life is filled with contradictions and dualities. We cannot imagine a world without joy and sorrow, birth and death, darkness and light. If we realize that joy and sorrow are the nature of the world, we would be even-minded while experiencing them.

A *sannyāsī* lived in a hut inside a village. He led a simple and pure life and the villagers respected him. The unmarried daughter of a village merchant became pregnant. At first, she refused to disclose the name of the child's father, but when her family coerced her, she named the sannyāsī. The young woman's father rebuked him harshly: "As you have brought dishonor to my daughter, you must take care of the child yourself!"

Hearing this, the sannyāsī replied without a trace of shame or anger, "Oh! Is that so?"

As soon as his daughter delivered the baby, the merchant entrusted it to the sannyāsī. When the villagers heard about this, they also started heaping abuse on him. But the sannyāsī did not pay much attention to them. He loved the baby and brought it up as if it were his own. A year passed. The young girl felt remorseful when she saw the sannyāsī being insulted for a lie she had uttered. Finally, she confessed that the neighbor's son had fathered the child. The merchant went to the sannyāsī and begged his pardon: "Please forgive us, who suspected and insulted you. We have come to take the child back."

The sannyāsī responded, "Oh! Is that so?"

Our true self is a source of peace that cannot be touched by any of the world's problems. Those who are established in their Self cannot see anything as other than themselves. They see the Supreme in all beings, moving and unmoving, and thus love and serve all of creation. They accept each and every situation with equanimity.

We must understand spirituality and make a conscious effort to reach this state of equal vision. Spirituality is the science of the mind. It teaches us not to become unsettled or distressed by the ups and downs of life and to remain joyful and content. This is the most important knowledge that we can gain in life.

Truth and Secrecy

Children, two things are important in worldly and spiritual life: truth and secrecy. Truth is the most important thing and must never be forsaken. Yet, there are truths we should not disclose to everyone. We must first consider the circumstances and the need. Before saying anything, we must consider three things carefully: One, whether what we are saying is true. If it is untrue, we must not speak it; two, whether it is useful. If it is not, we must not speak it; and three, whether it will hurt the ones who hear it. If it will, we must not speak it.

There are instances where the truth must be kept secret. For example, a woman might have done wrong in a moment of weakness. If the world knows about it, her future will be jeopardized. Her very life might be in danger. But if she keeps it a secret, she might be able to avoid repeating the mistake and lead a good life. Here, it is better to keep the truth secret than to disclose it, as we might be able to save a life and a family through this. This is why it is said that some things ought to be kept secret. But we can decide only after taking stock of the circumstances. Keeping it a secret should not motivate someone to repeat the mistake.

Let us take another example. A child died in an accident, which took place a hundred kilometers from her home. She was an only child. If her mother suddenly learns about her only child's death, she might also die of a broken heart. Therefore, this was what was said to her over the phone: "Your child met with a small accident and has been admitted to a nearby hospital. Come at once!" Even though this is a lie, it will give her the fortitude to hold up somehow until she has reached the hospital. At least during that interval, she can be spared the intense agony that she will experience soon. Maybe, during the time taken to travel to the hospital after hearing of her child's accident, some strength might have awakened in her, enabling her to face whatever is in store. When she hears the truth later, it will not be as shocking as it might have been had she been told suddenly. By concealing the truth for some time, another life can be saved. The dead child will never return to life, but why risk the life of another person? Amma is talking about such situations. White lies are not like other untruths.

We must never lie for our own advantage or to gain our own ends. It is equally important that we don't hurt another person through our words and actions. We might not be able to make anyone happy but we should at least not hurt them.

Speaking the truth and refraining from lying constitute the highest spiritual practice. When we utter a lie, we are betraying our conscience, the indwelling presence in us. That deed will manifest as an obstacle in our path. The words of those who always speak the truth will come true. Such people will attain the Truth.

Poverty

Children, poverty is the biggest challenge that humanity is facing today. The divide between the rich and the poor is increasing by the day. On one side is a towering mountain, and on the other, a gaping void. This is the state of the world now. A tiny percentage of humanity is leading a life of great luxury even as the vast majority are unable to make enough money to buy medicine or even a meal a day. They endure hunger and pain. A bridge made of love and compassion has to be built to connect the rich and the poor.

Poverty is a terrible calamity that destroys all the intrinsic goodness in people and inhibits all their potential. When Amma is on her overseas tours, children sometimes show her the pictures they draw and color. Once, a group of children brought pictures of warships, guns and bombs. One among them drew a picture of Christ with a gun in his hand. Upon inquiring about these children, Amma learnt that they came from the slums. Amma asked the boy who had drawn a picture of Christ with a gun, "Why did you draw a gun in Christ's hand?"

He said, "When Christ feels hungry, he'll need money. If he threatens someone with a gun, that person will give him money. Then Christ can eat!"

Amma asked him, "Will you get food only if you point a gun at someone?"

He answered, "Our father is raising us with money extorted from others at gunpoint."

"Why? Is he unhealthy and unable to work and earn a living?"

"No, father went to many places to look for work. But when people hear that he's from the slums, they don't want to give him a job. So, this is how our father is raising us."

Such experiences leave a deep impression on the young. Poverty and insecurity awaken violence in young minds. It is here that love and compassion are particularly relevant. If the rich, who constitute 10% of our population put their minds to it, they can uplift the 90% mired in poverty. If compassion awakens in them, poverty will end.

We don't need a lot of money to live comfortably. The wealthy must try their best to avoid luxuries and excesses. A ₹500 watch tells the time. Do we really need a ₹50,000 watch? Such extravagances will not give us true joy. Let us take only what we need and give the rest to those in dire need. Doing so will give us joy in the present and stay with us as *puṇya* (spiritual merit) in the future.

Corruption

Children, corruption is spreading in all fields of society today. It exists in one form or the other, not only in India, but all over the world. Usually, we talk only about financial corruption but exploiting nature, going to war, fomenting conflict, lying and manipulating people, and terrorism are all different forms of corruption because, in each instance, there has been a deviation from the straight path.

The fundamental reason for corruption is the widespread erosion of values in society. At present, we give more importance to solving the external causes of the problem than to acknowledging and tackling the weakening value system. Our unclean and crooked minds are responsible for corruption, cruelty and violence.

Greed has afflicted the world today with inner and outer blindness. Take as much as you can and in as many ways as you can—this thought has become entrenched in society's intellect. If the law and the government close one door, the greedy will find 10 other doors to open. In countries outside India, if you are caught driving above a certain speed, the police will impose a hefty fine. If you are caught speeding three times, your license will be revoked. That's how strict the rules are. That said, there are instruments fitted into almost every car that show where the police cars are waiting and where cameras are installed.

Likewise, if we are determined to amass wealth and make money in any way possible, we will discover new ways to make it.

To put an end to corruption, there must be laws without loopholes and technology that is secure. The police, the court and the government cannot be lenient in dealing with corruption. The media play a crucial role in clamping down on corruption, as they rouse the emotions of the masses and form public opinion. The media must neither cover up nor blow out of proportion cases of corruption. Instead, they must adopt an impartial and intrepid stand against corruption.

External solutions alone are not enough. There must be a transformation in our minds also. To bring this about, our education must give importance to spiritual values. Good and bad begin at home. Parents must be role models in word and deed for their children. Both at home and in school, we must try to create a culture that strengthens the values of mutual love, respect and trust, and compassion towards fellow beings and nature. Then, to a large extent, we can find a solution to the corruption pervading all walks of life.

In Praise of God

Children, one of the most important spiritual practices on the path of devotion is singing devotional songs and religious hymns that glorify God. Some might ask, "Doesn't this mean that God succumbs to praise?" God is not moved by outer praise. Both praise and insult are alike to Him. He will bless even those who hurl mud on Him; that's how compassionate He is.

It is true that the Purāṇas describe how God becomes pleased when hymns praising Him are sung. This does not mean that God likes being praised. When the gods got into trouble because of their egoism and carelessness, they fled to Vaikuṇṭha, the abode of Lord Viṣṇu, and took refuge in Him. They called out to Him many times but the Lord did not heed their call. Finally, a prayer arose from the depths of their hearts. Only then did the Lord open His eyes. Because the prayer came from the depths of their grieving hearts, they were able to gain a vision of the Lord within and without. Nothing pleases the Lord like innocent love. One cannot propitiate Him by praising Him for the sake of fulfilling one's selfish desires.

A merchant had two servants. The first was always calling out, "Master! Master," and trailing him. Though he was always praising the merchant's greatness, he never did any work. The second servant hardly ever came near the merchant. He was completely focused on finishing the tasks the merchant had assigned him. He would even forgo food and sleep to complete his work. Which servant is likely to be the merchant's favorite? The second, of course! God's grace flows more towards those who honor their dharma than to those who spend their lives merely calling out "God! God!" This does not mean that we need not praise God. We must praise Him and do good deeds as well. Only then will grace flow to us. Otherwise, our wrongdoing will destroy the goodness that heartfelt prayer invokes. It is like putting a heap of sugar on one side and placing an army of ants on the other. The ants will eat all the sugar!

The purpose of religious hymns and devotional songs is not to propitiate a God who wears a crown, has four arms, and lives in a heaven beyond the skies. The all-pervading God resides in our heart. Hymns and prayers are means to kindle this awareness. All hymns describe the form and glory of God, who is the embodiment of noble virtues such as love, compassion and patience. When we sing these hymns with an appreciation of their meaning, the love, compassion and patience of the Divine will grow in us. By praising God, we unknowingly becoming expansive in our outlook.

Giving

Children, the people of ancient India were so noble that they only took what they needed from their earnings and gave the rest away to the poor. But today, there are people who hoard wealth not only for themselves but for a thousand generations after them. At the same time, there are many poor people who cannot afford even one meal a day, but the hoarders don't understand this.

The intention behind every act of giving is to transform the selfish mind into a selfless one. Today, many give only nominally. They collect many one- and two-rupee coins and set this aside to give beggars when they go to places of pilgrimage. Surrender to God should not be confined to words alone. We ought to demonstrate it through our deeds. We must help the needy as much as we can. This is real worship, and it is the path to peace and contentment.

Amma is reminded of something she learnt while in school. A group of pilgrims were traveling to Rāmēśwaram after their pilgrimage to Kāśī. They were carrying with them pots of water from the Ganges to perform *abhiṣēka* (ceremonial bath) to Lord Śiva at Rāmēśwaram. To get there, the pilgrims had to cross a desert. There was no water to be found anywhere. They became terribly thirsty, and yet none of them wanted to use the holy water to quench their thirst. After a while, they came upon a donkey that had collapsed by the roadside, unable to bear the heat and thirst. One of the pilgrims felt sorry for the donkey, which was on the verge of death. He poured Ganga water from his pot into the donkey's mouth. The donkey eagerly gulped the water and was restored to life. The devotee felt happy that he had been able to save the donkey's life. But the other pilgrims accused him of committing heresy by pouring the holy water, meant for the abhiṣēka of Lord Śiva's idol, into a donkey's mouth. Hearing this, the pilgrim replied, "I don't mind if my pilgrimage becomes fruitless because I gave water to a dying animal. I see God even in that donkey. How can I pass by the dying animal without trying to quench its thirst?"

Four things give value to giving: sacrificing our own needs to give; giving selflessly without desiring anything, including name or fame, in return; giving to someone whose need is greater than ours; and giving with respect, seeing God in the recipient of our gift.

If we can cultivate the habit of giving to others in these ways, our life will be filled with contentment and abundance.

Sharing

Children, our society is racing against time. As a result, the culture and attitudes of people are changing gradually. Unfortunately, the tides of change are eroding our precious values and goodness. One of the eroding values is sharing, which was integral to village life.

If there were four houses adjacent to each other and if some tasty food was cooked in one home, that food would be shared among all four families. All the four families would do the same thing. They would share food, ideas, joys and sorrows and thus their hearts.

Amma recalls an incident that took place at the school where she studied. Most students were from families that earned their livelihood through fishing. Of these students, 10 to 15 would not have anything to eat for lunch. Some students would bring lunch with them to school, and those who lived nearby would go home for lunch. While those who brought lunch ate, the students without any food would sit on the veranda or elsewhere. One of the girls felt sad about this. She shared her lunch with one of the children who did not have any food. Seeing this, the other students who had brought food felt inspired to share their lunch with those without food. That day, no child went hungry. Then, the students who had gone home for lunch started coming back with packets of food for the students who did not have any food. The students in the other classes followed this example, and soon, no one in the school went hungry. The students who shared their food packets with others enjoyed their lunch more than the students who ate alone. The former realized that sharing was what made them content.

The girl's act of kindness brought about a transformation in the hearts of her schoolmates. Each one of us must also be ready to reserve some space for others in our hearts. It is kind hearts that bring about progress in society. If we have just a little love and compassion for others, we can bring great solace to others.

Even as we are borne along by the flow of life, let us not forget others. May each one of us be able to alleviate the sorrows and sufferings of others, and become a pillar of support for them.

Gṛhasthāśrama

Children, many of those who follow the spiritual path are householders. Family, relatives and friends are an important part of their lives. Many of them fear that their attachment to their near and dear ones may be an obstacle to making spiritual progress.

They can certainly advance on the spiritual path and attain God-realization. The only thing is, they must be dedicated to God. They must consider their responsibilities as God-given. A householder intent on God-realization has the attitude, "I have nothing of my own in this world. Everything belongs to God." If we have such an attitude, then our every action will become a worship of God and bring us closer to Him.

In ancient times, most Gurus were householders. Their goal in life was to realize God. They were brave renunciates. But householders today are consumed by thoughts of their spouse and children. They are not *gṛhasthāśramīs*, only *gṛhasthas.*[27]

A lion in a forest was getting married. Many lions gathered to celebrate the wedding. One group of lions was singing and

27 *Gṛhasthāśrama* is the second of the four *āśramas* or stages of life that Sanātana Dharma sanctions, the others being *brahmacarya* (life of a celibate student), *vānaprastha* (life of a retiree) and *sannyāsa* (life of renunciation). Regardless of which āśrama one lived in, the goal was the same: God-realization. Here, Amma is saying that the *gṛhastha* (householder) now doesn't have higher aspirations.

another was dancing. Among those dancing was a mouse. Seeing the mouse, a lion asked, "You're a mouse. What are you doing here?"

The mouse said, "I came for my younger brother's wedding."

"What?" said the Lion. "We're lions and you're a mouse. How can the lion groom be your younger brother?"

"I also used to be a lion. I became a mouse only after marriage!"

This should not be our fate. We should live with the goal of Self-realization uppermost in our mind.

We wade into the river to bathe. After bathing, we will go back ashore. We won't remain in the waters. Similarly, one enters into gṛhasthāśrama to overcome the obstacles on the path to God. Attachment arises from the sense of 'I' and 'mine.' We ought to regard the gṛhasthāśrama life as an opportunity to let go of this sense.

We ought to be like a bird perched on a dry twig. The bird will eat and sleep on it. But it is always alert, ready to fly off at any second, because it knows that the twig might snap at any moment. The world is also like a dry twig. It can abandon us at any time. While doing our duties in the world, let us not forget that they are ephemeral. We must always be ready to soar into the skies of the eternal self. Then nothing can bind us or make us unhappy.

Release from Sorrow

Children, life is full of problems. Though their causes might be many, we can group the problems under one of three categories: One, problems arising from natural forces; examples include earthquakes, gales, and sudden and torrential downpours. Two, problems arising from the world, society and living beings around us; these include epidemics, bothersome neighbors, mosquito bites, and the discomfort arising from sound and air pollution. Three, problems arising from within because of flaws in our character; they include jealousy, pride, hatred and prejudicial behavior.

The first two categories of problems are not always within our control. To a certain extent, we can control the problems arising from nature. But when nature becomes severely agitated, no one can withstand her fury. We can only hope to escape it. To an extent, we can also solve the second category of problems. For example, we can initiate a dialogue with our bothersome neighbor and hopefully come to an amicable solution. If not, we can complain to the police. We can use a mosquito repellant to keep the mosquitoes away. If we cannot tolerate the noise and air pollution from heavy traffic, we can move to another locality. But the third kind of problem is certainly within our control and we can solve them. If we try sincerely, we can correct the flaws in our character and behavior.

Our surroundings might be quiet and peaceful, but if our minds are not under our control, we will not experience peace and quiet. Conversely, if our minds are under our control, we can calmly face any problem in the world.

Whatever the problem is, the first step we must take to solve it is to find its real cause. When we face sorrow, we are often unable to see its real cause. We blame others, situations and even God. We forget that the true cause of our problems is within.

Once we discover the true cause of our problems, then finding solutions becomes much easier. Suppose a man is sad because he has been denied promotion. If he accepts his successes and failures equally and continues to work with renewed enthusiasm, he can solve this problem. Ninety percent of the problems in life occur because of shortcomings in our behavior and attitude. If we succeed in resolving these inadequacies, our life will become happier and more peaceful.

Action and Astrology

Children, many people turn to astrology when they are anxious or scared about their future. Many people worry about their marriage, business and promotions. The experience of happiness or sorrow is the consequence of our past actions. To an extent, astrology can give some indications of what is in store, but it cannot help us overcome the malefic effects of our past actions completely. Therefore, we must cultivate a mind that is capable of rising up to all the problems and challenges in life.

Once, a *mahātmā* (spiritually illumined soul) gave two statues to the king and said, "Take good care of these statues. When they break, disaster will strike the kingdom. War may break out, or the land might face a drought or flood."

The king entrusted the statues to one of his attendants, who kept them carefully in a safe place. One day, one of the statues broke. When the attendant reported the matter, the furious king had him imprisoned. A few days later, a neighboring king and his vast forces attacked the kingdom. The king's anger boiled over and he ordered the attendant to be hanged. Before being led to the gallows, the attendant was asked if he had any final wish. He said, "Before I die, allow me to break the second statue also."

Hearing this, the king asked, "Why do you make such a request?"

The attendant replied, "You sentenced me to death for breaking one statue. If the other statue breaks, another innocent man will also have to die. The mahātmā who gave you these statues said that when they break, the country would face hard times. He did not say that the hard times would come *because* the statues break but *when* they break. The breaking of the statue was an indication of impending war. As soon as this indication made itself known, you ought to have prepared our army to face the enemy."

The king realized his mistake, released the attendant, and absolved him of all wrongdoing.

Horoscopes and inauspicious signs can only give us an indication of the joys and sorrows coming our way. But it is futile to blame God or the planets for our suffering. We must try to perform good deeds in the present. Then, our future will be bright.

Amma is not saying that we shouldn't try to avoid adverse circumstances. But if we don't succeed even after striving sincerely, we should try to gain the mental strength to accept it as God's will. Then, there will be peace and contentment in life.

Water, Our Wealth.

Children, in many houses these days, one can see wallpapers featuring beautiful natural scenes or such pictures mounted on the walls. This clearly indicates that the people in those homes love nature. Yet, people still fell trees, destroy sacred groves, and fill in ponds. Only if we protect nature can we conserve our precious water, and vice versa.

Today, the water on earth is drying up. In the olden days, no one would have thought even in their wildest dreams that water levels on earth would decline. And yet, people then were careful not to waste water. They knew that without water, there can be no life or living. In those days, in all homes, people would fill up *kiṇḍis*[28] with water. They would wash their hands and feet with water from kiṇḍis. Thus, not even a single drop of water would be wasted. Today, many people don't even bother to turn off the tap properly after using it.

Amma is reminded of her childhood. There used to be only one water pipe in the village. Only if we stood in line at this pipe early in the morning would we be able to fill a pot of water by night. Sometimes, we wouldn't get any water. As a result of growing up under such circumstances, even now, if Amma sees a leaking water pipe while traveling somewhere, Amma will become upset, as if her own body were bleeding. Amma will immediately stop the car, get out and try to find a way to plug

28 *Pitchers with a narrow spout.*

the leak. Amma has this attitude because she realized the value of water at a young age.

Today, most of the rains falling in Kerala flow into the sea. Therefore, even if you have just five *cents* of land (about 2,178 square feet), you must set aside half or a quarter of it to create a pond. Those without sufficient space can build rainwater harvesting tanks right next to their house.

In the old days, there used to be groves adjoining every house. In due course, people began to consider the necessity of having such groves blind faith, and destroyed these groves, with the result that the air and water lost their purity. There ought to be a small grove beside every house where trees such as the fig, banyan, peepul and the like can be planted. May we be able to implement such good practices, which our ancestors bequeathed us.

Each one of us must do our best to protect our water sources and not waste water. We must teach children to open the taps only a little while using them. Only if everyone awakens and acts concertedly can humanity continue to survive.

Cleanliness

Children, there was a time when the Third World War was considered the greatest threat to humanity. But today environmental pollution has assumed far more threatening proportions. The soil, water and air on earth have become polluted.

With the growth of cities and the proliferation of industries, the population in cities has increased. Waste is accumulating in huge piles. We must find scientific ways to dispose of it properly. Otherwise, the environment will become polluted and epidemics will spread. Building hospitals and discovering new medicines are not solutions to these problems.

We mustn't discard waste carelessly while cleaning the house and yard. We must try to reuse waste. First, we must sort waste into biodegradable and plastic waste. We can use biodegradable waste to make organic compost, which is very good for farming. We can clean and reuse plastic waste in many ways. For example, we can make bags, baskets, mats and other objects of daily use. We must reuse such waste creatively. We must also create an awareness in society about cleanliness and on processing and reusing waste.

Once, a minister was invited to a village to inaugurate Cleanliness Week. He reached the village the night before the inauguration. When the organizers went to meet him the next day, he was nowhere to be seen. They went in search of him and found him sweeping the streets of the village. Seeing this, the villagers started to help him. The cleaning became like a festival. By the time of the inauguration, the whole village had been swept clean. It is not words but actions that are important. Instead of talking about noble principles, we must walk the talk. People will be able to assimilate principles easily when we teach them through example.

In the old days, there was no particular need for environmental protection because protecting the environment was a part of everyday life. People saw the Creator in creation, and loved and served nature and all other living beings. We must try to awaken this attitude once again.

The mental and physical health of the mother affects the health of the children also. If the mother is happy and eats nutritious food, her children will be benefitted through her breast milk and tender love. Likewise, if Mother Nature remains healthy, the air we breathe, the water we drink, and the food we eat will be pure and nutritious. If we can protect nature and stop polluting it, the coming generations will benefit from our actions.

Nature Conservation

1

Children, human beings are losing sleep today over natural disasters and climatic changes. The balance and harmony in nature have been disturbed by our thoughtless exploitation of natural resources. The air, water and soil have become toxic.

Long ago, human beings traveled in bullock and horse carts. Then we started traveling on motorbikes and in cars. Now, some people even have two or three cars. As a result, fuel is becoming scarce. Earlier, we used to eat off plates made from leaves. Today, we use paper plates and cups. After just one use, we discard them. How many trees have to be cut down to make paper utensils! Nature is being exploited and her resources misused because of our attachment to pleasure.

Nature, which was like Kāmadhēnu, the divine, wish-fulfilling cow, has now become like an emaciated cow that has stopped producing milk. The number of forests on earth is decreasing. There is less food. It is becoming difficult to find pure air and water. Diseases are increasing.

Where did we go wrong? We failed to distinguish between need and luxury. Even if it is a legitimate need, taking more than we need from nature is unethical and sinful.

Amma is reminded of the story of a social worker. One morning, he took a pot of water from the river to use for brushing his teeth. While brushing his teeth, he spoke to his colleagues about certain important matters. When he lifted the pot to rinse his mouth, he realized that there was no water in it. He said, "O God! I've been so careless that I used up the water before I finished brushing my teeth."

His colleagues did not understand the reason for his anguish. They asked him, "Why are you so upset? Don't you see the river flowing right in front of you?"

The man said, "It's true that there is water in the river. But I don't have the right to take more than I need."

If the present generation can regain the dharmic consciousness that this social worker demonstrated, there will be no deaths caused by starvation and poverty.

We should take from nature only what we need for our sustenance. Then, there will be enough water, food and clothing for everyone. Nature will once again become like Kāmadhēnu.

A scientist once said, "If all the insects were to disappear from the earth, within 50 years, all life on earth would end. If all human beings disappeared from earth, within 50 years all forms of life would flourish." May it never come to pass that we must cease to be for earth to survive.

This world, which our ancestors bequeathed to us, is indeed beautiful. Are we going to make a mess of it before passing it on to future generations? It is our duty to ensure that we leave the earth to future generations without so much as a scratch on it.

We have the responsibility to protect Mother Nature as we would our own mother. Let us open our eyes to this truth. Actually, it is not our responsibility to nature but to humankind, because without nature, we cannot survive.

2

Children, the greatest challenge that humankind is facing today is the population explosion. Day by day, the number of human beings in the world is growing. But natural resources have not increased proportionately. On the contrary, they are getting depleted. Any development that disregards nature paves the way to rampant pollution. Fields have become contaminated by poisonous chemicals. Ponds, rivers and sacred groves have been destroyed. Pure food, water and air are no longer available.

There is no other solution to these problems than to curtail our use of natural resources. At present, we use items such as pens, pencils and paper and then discard them. We must try to reuse them.

Everything in nature has its own purpose. We must find out what it is before using it. Then we will see that there is no such thing as waste. Organic waste can be turned into organic compost. If we try, we can also find creative ways to reuse old paper and plastic.

Once, a disciple asked the Buddha for a new set of robes, as his old ones had become tattered. Permission was granted. The next day, the Buddha asked the disciple, "Did you get new robes? Do you need anything else?"

The disciple said, "Yes, Master, I did. Thank you. I don't need anything else."

Buddha: What did you do with the old robes?

Disciple: I'm using them as bedsheets.

Buddha: Did you throw away the old sheets?

Disciple: No, I'm using them as curtains for my window.

Buddha: What did you do with the old curtains?

Disciple: I'm using them to hold hot vessels in the kitchen.

Buddha: What did you do with the cloths that had been used to hold the hot vessels?

Disciple: They are being used to wipe the floor.

Buddha: What happened to the rags that were being used to wipe the floor?

Disciple: Master, they have become threadbare. As they can't be used for anything else, we have made wicks out of them.

Hearing these words, the Buddha smiled gently.

This story teaches us that we can find some use even for objects we consider useless.

Let us use natural resources in moderation, and try as far as possible to reuse items. If we do so, we can create a waste-free world. May that be our goal.

3

Children, we are living at a critical time when environmental problems have reached a tipping point. Our thoughtless actions have polluted the soil, water and air. We have destroyed nature by cutting trees down, bulldozing mountains, and mining sand from riverbeds. Today, we are facing the consequences of our actions. Before suffering from a heart attack, the body shows indications of the impending attack. Likewise, each natural disaster is a warning from Mother Nature to correct our actions.

Once, a hunter released a poisoned arrow aimed at a herd of deer. The arrow missed its target and hit a huge tree with widely spread-out branches. The arrow's poisoned tip became wedged in its trunk. The strong poison started killing the tree. It became black and withered and shed all its leaves. Birds, squirrels and other animals abandoned it. But a parrot continued living there out of gratitude and love for the dying tree. It stopped eating and sleeping, and remained perched there, grieving. Friends tried to cajole the parrot to abandon the tree and find a new home, but the parrot did not yield. This wondrous news spread throughout the three worlds and reached the ears of Dēvēndra, the chief of the gods. He decided to test the parrot's love and gratitude for the tree.

Dēvēndra came to the parrot in the guise of an old Brāhmin and asked, "Why don't you abandon this withered tree?"

The parrot said, "By the power gained from practicing spiritual austerities, I recognize you as Dēvēndra. I was born in this tree. It was while living here that I acquired all my virtues and skills. I depended on it to protect myself when my enemies attacked me. How can I now abandon this tree, which has nourished and protected me all my life?"

Hearing this, Dēvēndra said, "I am pleased with your compassion. Ask me for a boon." The parrot asked Dēvēndra to restore the tree to its previous grandeur. Dēvēndra rained immortal nectar on the tree. Within moments, the tree was revived. Green and lustrous leaves sprouted, weaving a thick canopy on the tree's branches. Fruits hung low from it. Seeing this, the birds, insects, squirrels and other animals that had abandoned it returned joyfully and resumed staying there.

If we have the same bond with and gratitude to nature that the parrot had, protecting nature will become easy. May we be able to impart this culture of environmental protection to the new generation.

4

Children, man, who has been exploiting nature to enhance his own comforts, has now become a threat to the very existence of life on this planet. Man is not separate from but a part of nature. His very existence depends on nature. If natural rhythms go awry, man will lose the rhythm in his life.

There is a saying, "If you cut down a tree, you must plant 10 saplings." But even this is not sufficient. Ten saplings cannot provide the coolness that a tree does. They don't have the same purifying effect on the atmosphere that a tree has. They cannot contribute as much to the harmony of nature.

Man is encroaching upon and destroying nature. Many species have become extinct. If we are not careful, extinction will soon become our fate too.

Traditional beliefs and values play a major role in protecting nature. Once, during her North Indian tour, Amma visited a pilgrimage center. Thousands of years ago, a *mahātmā* (spiritually illumined soul) had sat and meditated under a peepul tree and attained spiritual liberation. Now, there is huge tree descended from the original peepul tree there. Hundreds of devotees and pilgrims circumambulate the tree reverentially and pray devoutly. When dry leaves fall to the ground, the devotees rush to pick them up. If someone obtains even one leaf, she will hold it close to her heart with much devotion. After fervently thanking God, she will carefully keep the leaf safely inside her bag. If only we cherish all the trees in the world with the same love and reverence that these devotees show the peepul tree, our world will be a thousand times more beautiful.

Our ancestors did not see the sun as an inert globe. They regarded and worshipped it as God. They saw the Earth as a Goddess. They had tremendous respect for rivers, mountains and trees. How is it possible for someone who worships rivers as sacred waterbodies to pollute them with toxic chemicals? How can a society that worships trees as demi-gods decimate forests? Let us reawaken those age-old values that protected and conserved nature. May we be able to revive a culture that sees God in all of nature and thus serve and protect her.

God Created Villages; Man Created Cities.

Talking about the state of Kerala today, Amma is reminded of a man who achieved great success in life. Reporters asked him, "What's the secret of your success?"

"Two words."

"What are those two words?"

"Right decisions."

"How could you make the right decisions all the time?"

"One word."

"What is it?"

"Experience."

"How did you gain that experience?"

"Two words: wrong decisions." With that, he ended the interview.

We call Kerala 'God's own country.' Kerala is beautiful. Mountains, forests, rivers and lush greenery endow Kerala with natural beauty. But today, Kerala's beautiful face is becoming distorted even as we speak. We are now experiencing the consequences of our wrong decisions and actions. If Keralites do not learn from these experiences and make the right decisions and do the right things, heaven on earth will soon become hell on earth.

It is said, "God created villages; man created cities." In God's creation, there is an order to everything and a place for all beings. Forests, rivers and mountains—each has its own dharma or intrinsic nature. Nature has provided enough to sustain all living beings. Nature has the ability to recycle and reuse the waste it produces to protect itself. Thus, nature has an inbuilt mechanism for protecting the environment. When we exploit natural resources rampantly for our selfish ends, the natural harmony and rhythm become disturbed. Nature's face becomes distorted. We must face the consequences of our actions.

Cities and factories came into existence as a result of scientific progress. Some cities became overpopulated. Waste dumps were created. If we do not find a scientific and environmentally friendly way to treat the waste, nature will become polluted. Epidemics will spread. Building hospitals and discovering new medicines are not solutions. Today, everything is contaminated. Even the air, water and food have become toxic. Poison enters our food not only through chemical fertilizers but also through food that is adulterated to satisfy our greed. The earth is drying up because forests are being razed. Rivers are drying up and becoming small streams. The face of cities is being mutilated by assorted waste, rotting fruit peels, discarded bottles and cigarette butts.

We must learn the right lessons from these experiences. If we are still not ready to change our ways, nature will teach us a good lesson. We may not be able to handle that blow. Mother Nature has already blessed us by giving us all that we need. But if we forget our *dharma* (duty) and, like runaway horses, let loose the reins of our desires, nature will retaliate. Blessings will become curses. Therefore, let us not delay making the right decisions and taking the right actions. They must be implemented at every level. Discussions must be held at the individual and governmental levels and with relevant organizations on how to solve our environmental problems. Both personal and collective efforts are needed. Our thinking usually remains at the levels of the intellect and logic. We should also think of spiritual solutions. Trying to keep spiritual thought away from society is one of the main causes of many problems we face today. In many foreign countries, there is cleanliness but no values. That is the problem they face. Only when we equate cleanliness to Godliness will we attain perfection.

We must impart lessons on cleanliness to children from childhood. They must be trained to keep their homes and surroundings neat and tidy and not to discard waste carelessly. They must be given this training at home and in school. The subject of environmental protection must be included in the school syllabi. Children must also be guided practically on how to love and take compassionate care of nature.

We teach students about the world and worldly affairs, but we have forgotten to teach them about love and compassion, which are the foundation of life. Along with knowledge of the external world, we must also learn to give and accept love. When knowledge and love that is rooted in spirituality go hand in hand, we will love all beings. We will protect nature. We will keep the environment clean. This will usher in a new tomorrow.

The World is One Family

Children, this world is one family and we are all its members. When those who live under one roof discharge their responsibilities with the sense of being part of one family, peace and unity will prevail. We should not think of ourselves solely as members of a particular race or country. Only if we live and act with the awareness that we are members of a global family will peace and contentment dawn on earth.

When Amma travels throughout the world, many people come to tell her their sorrows. One woman said, "Amma, some men came and stabbed my husband to death." Other people lament, "Amma, rioters reduce our homes to ashes." Amma has had to hear many such heart-wrenching tales. The conflict might be between different religions or sects, between races or between countries. Amma feels sad whenever she hears such accounts. It is all right to believe in any religion or be a citizen of any country but we should not forget our own humanity or forsake humane values in the name of religion or country.

There was a big lake between two countries. Because of disputes over who owned the lake, the two countries became enemies. That did not stop the people of either country from sailing on the lake. One day, there was a severe storm and many sailboats capsized. When one man was drowning, another man swam to him and helped him reach the shore safely. They embraced each other and asked each other's name and neighborhood. When they realized that they were from opposing countries, they became hostile towards each other. Earlier, when there had been no such thoughts, they had been conscious only of their shared humanity and not of their differing national identities. But when they learnt that they were from enemy nations, they lost that sense of love and oneness, and became bitter and angry with each other.

We should never forget that, over and above everything else, we are human beings. Only then do we become members of any religion or country. So, our foremost duty is to protect our humanity. The allegiance we have towards any particular religion, country or sect must never lead us to forsake the values that make us human.

The World is a Mirror

Children, most of us expect love and respect from others but forget that they also expect the same things from us. The world is like a mirror. If we smile at a mirror, our reflection will smile back at us. If we grimace, we will get a grimace in return. We get back what we offer the world.

A doctor was transferred to a government hospital in a village. His conduct was very pleasing. Nothing ruffled his calm demeanor—neither the hectic pace of hospital life nor the behavior of patients. Seeing this, a man asked the doctor, "How can you keep smiling even amidst so many patients?"

The doctor said, "Life taught me a valuable lesson. Earlier, I used to work in a private hospital. I would travel by bus to work. I would wait for the bus at the bus stop, but invariably, the bus would stop some distance away. By the time I ran to the bus, it would have left without me. If I somehow managed to board the bus, there would be no seats available. Often, after I paid the fare, the bus conductor would not give me my change. If I asked him for it, he would give me the change angrily. By then, I would have lost all control over my mind and would reach the hospital with pent-up anger. I would not be able to smile at my colleagues or pay proper attention to my work. Then, the senior doctor would scold me. I would carry this stress home and vent all my frustration and distress there. Because of this, I became isolated both at home and at work.

"One day, when I reached the bus stop, the bus had just started moving. Seeing me, the conductor rang the bell and stopped the bus. There was no seat available on the bus. The conductor got up from his seat and asked me to sit there. I don't have the words to explain how much relief the conductor's behavior gave me. When I reached the hospital, I felt that everyone was smiling at me. That day, I was able to work attentively, and the senior doctor praised me. When I reached home, I was loving towards my wife and children. I became aware of the transformation that had taken place within me because of the conductor's behavior towards me. I also noticed how the behavior of others changed towards me. I vowed then to behave lovingly to others always."

Our every smile, word and deed have the power to bring light into the lives of many people. We must try to behave in such a way that we bring happiness and fulfilment to ourselves and others.

Develop Villages

Children, the vast majority of our population lives in villages. We consume the grains, vegetables and fruits grown by village farmers. Villages are the cradle of India's culture. But they are now in danger. When agriculture ceased to be profitable, villagers became poor. Suicides among farmers are on the rise, as is unemployment. Many of the youth are migrating to cities.

Most villages have seen nothing of development. They have very few roads that are fit for travel. There are not enough hospitals and schools. People are suffering because they are not even able to get drinking water. But the biggest problem is the erosion of values among people. There used to be love, unity and cooperation among villagers. Neighborly bonds were strong. They would share what they earned daily with each other and led contented lives. Even when they faced poverty, villagers adhered to values.

Amma is reminded of a story. Once two farmers went to a judge. One of them complained, "I bought some land from this man. While ploughing the field yesterday, I unearthed a copper pot filled with gold coins and precious jewels. As I bought only his land and not the gold coins and jewels, I asked him to take the treasure. But he is refusing to do so. Please help us solve this problem."

The second man said, "He is speaking the truth. But how can I accept the treasure? When I sold him the land, I gave everything in it to him. Now, he's forcing me to take the treasure. Please save me from his nuisance."

The judge was pleased with their honesty and self-sacrificing attitude. But he had to solve the problem somehow. He asked the two farmers many questions and understood that one of them had a daughter of marriageable age whereas the other had an unmarried son. After some thought, the judge said, "Let your children marry each other. This treasure should be gifted to them after their marriage." Thus, the plaintiff and the defendant left as relatives.

Our villages have always safeguarded our culture and values. Because of their heartfelt bond with the land and with nature, villagers were able to retain and uphold our culture. But now, values are eroding even in villages. Vices like alcoholism have plunged villagers into misery.

India will progress only when her villages develop. When we work with the aim of developing our villages, we must take care not to destroy their innate beauty, which resides in the innocence of the villagers, their simplicity and culture. It is our responsibility to preserve the traditional culture and value systems of the villagers even as we bring economic progress into the villages.

We can do many things to improve the current situation in the villages. We can provide vocational training to unemployed youth, both boys and girls. We can teach the illiterate how to read and write. We can adopt scientific methods to rehabilitate those who are addicted to alcohol and drugs. We can do many such things. By doing so, we can make our villages prosperous once again.

Violence and Conflict

Children, the conflict between good and evil is age-old. Since time immemorial, there have been wars between the gods and demons. Many *avatārs* (divine incarnations) and *mahātmās* (spiritually illumined souls) have worked tirelessly for the good of this world. Yet, there doesn't seem to be any improvement, as wars and conflicts continue to this day. Can there ever be a lasting solution to this? Some people ask, "Why is it that even illumined souls have not been able to bring about any change in the world?"

The wars and conflicts that we see in the world are a manifestation of the battles raging in our minds. The mind is our best friend and our worst enemy. The mind has the capacity to uplift or destroy us. If we can gain control over the mind and use it well, we can help to uplift humanity. Otherwise, the mind will bring about total annihilation. In truth, the mind ought to be an obedient servant. But at present, it is our master, lording over us. As long as ego and selfishness reign, there will continue to be war and conflict. It has more or less always been like this.

Mahātmās are our guiding lights. By living lives of renunciation and compassion, they have become role models inspiring people. We must be prepared to travel along the path they illuminate. The world has been sustained only by the presence and noble deeds of mahātmās. If not for them, things would have been far worse. There are people who ask, "What's the use of having a police force, an army and laws? There has been no let-up in corruption and violence." But let us not forget that it is only because of them that conditions have not deteriorated any further.

Man can become Rāma or Rāvaṇa. The forces of both good and evil are within. We must decide which to use and how to use it. It is the nature of the mind to flow down whereas spirituality teaches us how to uplift the mind. When the mind flows down, its power manifests as desire, anger, jealousy and the like. If we can give this power an upward boost, the same mind will express the sacred and transformative power of divine love.

We can learn lessons from the evil that we see around us. When we see someone doing wrong, we must activate our conscience and resolve to not do the same thing.

When we see someone doing wrong, we must learn to not be like that person, and when we see someone doing good, we must learn to be like him or her. If we can imbibe these lessons, our lives and the society we live in will become peaceful.

Why Study the Scriptures?

Children, quite a few people say that those who study religious or scriptural texts become big-headed and arrogant. But Amma feels that those who have studied them properly become humble and are able to understand others. If anyone with only a superficial knowledge of the scriptures thinks, "I'm knowledgeable. So, what I say is right. Everyone else is ignorant," then that person is the biggest ignoramus. It is good to study the dharma texts. But if they are not understood correctly, we will become more egoistic, and this will prove dangerous to us and others.

To understand the essence of the scriptures, the mind must become meditative. Unless one contemplates the teachings deeply, one will become more confused, as mere intellectual knowledge only creates unwanted thoughts, which will gradually lead to wrong knowledge and confusion. That is why the spiritual masters say that scriptural study and meditation must go hand in hand. This is true not only for spiritual knowledge. Meditation is needed to acquire material knowledge also.

To gain clarity in our thoughts and viewpoints, we must be able to curb our thoughts to some extent and still the mind. Many study hard so as to score high marks in their exams. They study day and night, and commit everything to memory. They might gain high marks and good grades. But they might not succeed in life. Others might be the ones who discover new ideas and ways to implement them. Even though they might not have scored high marks in exams, they succeed in life. There is a difference between acquiring knowledge and making practical use of it.

Studying the scriptures is not only about becoming proficient in Sanskrit and learning certain words and phrases by heart. Scriptural statements became illumined in the hearts of sages when they were absorbed in a state of profound meditation. Only a student whose mind has become subtle can understand the meaning and depth of those statements. This subtlety can be achieved only through contemplation and meditation.

God-realization is the highest experience. Everyone has small or big experiences in their lives. Poets, artists, scientists, entrepreneurs, politicians, sweepers and scavengers sometimes gain insights through modest experiences. But these experiences are transient. The world they illuminate is also narrow. But the ultimate spiritual experience reveals the secrets of the whole universe. Scriptural study alone cannot give one such a sublime experience. Along with scriptural study, one must constantly practice stilling the mind.

The mind and thoughts are impediments to spiritual experiences. For example, to enjoy the beauty of a flower, we must put aside our interpretations about the flower. But just one look with a quiet mind will suffice to appreciate the beauty of the flower in all its totality. Similarly, only when the mind is silent can we understand scriptural truths and assimilate them properly. Only in a still mind are the meanings of scriptural statements wholly revealed.

Once, a young man approached a *mahātmā* (spiritually illumined soul) and requested to be accepted as a disciple. The mahātmā said, “Write down all that you know about religion and spirituality, and bring it back to me. This will be an excellent practice for you.”

The youth did as he was instructed and started noting down all that he knew. A year later, he returned with a fat book in his hand. “Although I have filled all the pages of this book, I haven’t been able write down everything that I know about religion and spirituality. Please go through the book and give me your comments.”

The Guru took the book, skimmed through its pages, and said, “Good! Even though you took quite some time, this book is both simple and subtle. But it’s too long. Can you make it shorter?”

Five years later, the disciple reappeared with a book half the size of the first. The Guru looked through the book and said encouragingly, “This is very good! You have included almost everything in it. The writing is also clear and beautiful. But it’s still too long. Make it shorter. Put down only the essence of spirituality, and bring it back to me.”

Although the disciple felt a little discouraged by the Guru’s response, he wanted to obey the Guru. Ten years later, the disciple returned with a five-page leaflet and told the Guru, “This is the essence of my spiritual quest. It expresses the foundation and meaning of life. I will always be indebted to you for helping me understand this.”

The Guru carefully went through each line and each page and offered his heartfelt congratulations. He then said, “This is the crystallization of your contemplation, spiritual practices and austerities. But even this is still not perfect. You must make this even clearer."

Years passed. The Guru's life was drawing to a close. The disciple arrived, prostrated before the Guru, and handed him a blank sheet of paper; there was nothing written on it. He then begged the Guru to bless him. With great joy, the Guru placed his hand on the disciple's head and said, "Now you truly know everything."

The disciple stood silently in front of his Guru and bowed down to him. At that moment, the Guru left his mortal body.

Children, only when the awareness that "I am nothing! I know nothing!" arises, will supreme knowledge dawn in us. Ever remain a child in the world of knowledge. Always remain a beginner. When we study the scriptures with this attitude, their real meaning will be revealed spontaneously from within. Gradually, this will lead us to God-realization.

Education

1

The desire to know is in everyone. From the moment we are born, we start gathering knowledge. We must be able to distinguish between what is good and bad, what is beneficial and what isn't, and take in only what is necessary. This is the purpose of education. It ought to refine our character, hone our talents, give us a civic consciousness, and uplift us spiritually.

A porter uses his head to carry heavy loads whereas a scientist uses his to make new discoveries. Though there is infinite power within all of us, many of us are not aware of it. We must awaken this power lying dormant within us. This is the real objective of education.

God has given everyone different aptitudes and talents. Through effort, we can develop them. In fact, we can accomplish anything through one-pointed focus, enthusiasm and discipline.

Discipline alone will take our life to a higher level. A knife will rust if we don't use it daily. But if we do, it won't. Similarly, if we polish our mind daily, our talents will blossom.

It is good for students to wake up before sunrise. Doing so will make them healthy and enthusiastic. The pre-dawn hours are also ideal for meditating and studying.

After bathing early in the morning, children must pray and meditate for at least 15 minutes. Then they will be able to study better. All our talents are God-given.

Prostrating to one's parents before leaving for school is a good habit. We have heard of the saying, '*Mātā pitā guru daivam*'—'Mother, father, teacher, God.' What this means is that our first Guru is our mother. Then comes the father. After that come our teachers. In fact, all of nature is our Guru. We can learn from even the smallest creature. We can learn from an ant and a cow. The whole of nature is a book for us to study.

It is not enough for education to improve our standard of living. It must also help us uphold values. Student life is an opportunity to learn the lessons that can help us live a good life. We can learn lessons that are more important than science, mathematics and English: friendship; helping each other; compassion; discipline; obedience; respecting elders; patience; speaking kind words; not wasting food and water; and many other lessons besides. We can learn not only from teachers but also from friends. We can learn to think for ourselves and thus learn many things on our own. In fact, we must maintain the enthusiasm to learn throughout life. We must not become disheartened when we encounter small setbacks. We can also learn from failure and move on. If we are attentive, enthusiastic and patient, we will never fail anywhere.

2

Children, in the old days, spirituality was given great importance in India. But its place has been usurped by materialism. There is no point in thinking that we can bring back the old ways.

Such attempts will lead only to disappointment. We must think about how we can move forward in these altered circumstances without harming what is noble in our culture.

In the earlier days, children were sent to school when they were five years old. Today, they are being sent to nurseries when they are just two-and-a-half. Until the age of five, children must be loved. Their freedom should not be curtailed in any way. They should be able to play as they please. We only need to ensure that they don't jump into lakes or fire. Even when they are mischievous, we must express only love to them. When we point out their mistakes, we should do so affectionately. Children should be raised until the age of five in a cocoon of love, akin to the mother's womb.

Nowadays, in the name of education, we are placing a heavy burden on children, one that is more than they can bear. Like caged birds, we are shackling small children to their classrooms at a time they ought to spend in fun and games. Parents get upset if their children don't top their class even in kindergarten. As a result, children become tense and suffer.

Children live in a world of innocence. They grow up telling stories to flowers and butterflies and look with wonder at the world around them. They enjoy the world around them and spread their happiness to others. But the elders do not appreciate their innocence. Instead, they are eager to drag the children into the world of competition and conflict.

Amma is reminded of a story. Two children from neighboring houses were playing with each other. While playing, one child's hand was slightly injured. Seeing this, his mother angrily remonstrated with the mother of the first child. The mothers began arguing, and soon their husbands and other neighbors joined in and took sides. The quarrel almost blew up into a fight. In the meantime, someone went to look for the children and found them laughing and playing with each other. They had forgotten their tiff.

Parents don't advise their children to understand the goal of life and to live in accordance with it. Nobody tries to understand the children's aptitude and encourage it. If competition is healthy, it will help the children do better in their studies and bring out their talents. But today, competition often stresses students. If they don't do as well as they had hoped in the exams, they become depressed. They could remain dispirited for the rest of their lives.

Children, reflect on the purpose of education. It is true that modern education gives us a degree and enables us to find highly paid jobs. But can we gain peace of mind? We must impart values to our children. Otherwise, instead of a Rāma, we would be raising a Rāvaṇa. The values to which our minds are attuned create the foundation for peace and well-being in life. We can gain the ideal values only through spirituality.

3

Children, India was once the pride of the world on account of her learning and culture. In those days, students from all over the globe came here for higher studies. Somehow, the tide of time dislodged India from her position. But if we put our mind to it, we can progress and regain our former glory. Alongside spirituality and culture, we must also progress economically. Students must grow in knowledge, discernment and humility.

We must awaken their curiosity. Children must be trained to study, inquire and think independently.

With this goal in mind, we must give more importance to research. Schools should become well-equipped. The bond between teacher and student must be strong. If we take care of these things, India can soon regain its lost prestige in the field of science. But material progress alone isn't enough. Our country's growth and development must be aligned without our culture and values. The lowest strata of society also must benefit from the country's development.

Amma has a request. All universities should send their students to impoverished rural villages for at least a two-month internship. When the youth work in these villages, they will be able to interact with the poor, and witness their troubles and sorrows firsthand. Compassion will awaken in the hearts of the youth. Later, when they wish to spend money on unnecessary luxuries, they will remember those villagers. They will be more inclined to avoid luxury and to lead a simpler life, and feel motivated to use the money saved for the welfare of the poor and needy. They will also try to solve the problems that villagers face, with the scientific and technological skills acquired in the university. This will help to raise the standard of living in the villages.

In universities, the success of research is usually assessed on the basis of how much funding is received and the number of papers published in journals. But we must also consider how useful the research is to society or to what extent it has benefitted those living in the lowest strata of society. This ought to be the yardstick by which excellence in research is measured.

The aim of education is not just to help us understand the language of machines. If education is to become complete, we must also gain good values. We must also understand the language of the heart, the language of compassion.

Love, Patience and Faith.

Children, the doors of infinite possibilities are always open to us. We can enter them and travel as far as we wish. The vast skies of knowledge and strength can become our very own.

We have the capacity to be whatever we want to be. We can be noble beings who, through our thoughts and deeds, want only good for everyone. Or we can be the very epitome of evil. We can become divine or demonic. We have the freedom to determine what we wish to be. This is the uniqueness and blessing of a human life. But to avail of this blessing, we must have childlike faith and innocence.

Many of us blindly oppose and criticize anything that the brain cannot measure or evaluate. We often forget that faith and innocent love have the power to uplift us to realms that the intellect and logic cannot reach. Actually, we can see the power of innocence behind the discoveries that many great scientists have made. Have you seen a baby's eyes? They look at everything with innocent wonder. Likewise, a true scientist also views this universe with wonder. It is this attitude that leads him or her into the mysteries of the universe. A toddler falls down many times before learning how to walk. He might injure his hands, legs and forehead and even bleed. But nothing deters him from trying to walk. In children, we can see the most striking examples of self-confidence and faith in the efficacy of effort.

We often try to appraise life solely on the basis of our intellect and logic. But in doing so, we might not be able to plumb the depths of knowledge and experience. We must approach life and its experiences with love and faith. Only then will life reveal its secrets to us. Life is not just mathematics, science or spiritual principles. It is a mystery. To learn its secrets, we need love, patience and faith more than intelligence and logic. This is what spirituality teaches.

Our society considers people who question anything and everything to be intellectuals. Amma is reminded of a story. There was a village youth whom everyone considered a fool right from his boyhood. Whenever he said or did anything, his father would call out, "Fool!" His mother and siblings also did the same thing. Hearing this, his neighbors and other villagers also started calling him a fool. The poor lad thought, "I must be a fool. That's why everyone calls me one." Nevertheless, he kept trying to prove that he was intelligent, in vain. He was considered worthless at home and in his village. The lad became sad and disappointed.

At that point in time, a *mahātmā* (spiritually illumined soul) visited the village. The lad opened up and told him how sad he was. The mahātmā consoled him, "Don't be sad. From now on, whatever anyone says, talk back, opposing that person's viewpoint. For example, if someone says 'Look at that flower. It's so beautiful!' You should immediately say, 'Ugh! Who said it was? Can you prove it?' Or suppose someone talks about the greatness of love. You must immediately retort 'Love? There is nothing like that. Don't talk nonsense. Where proof is there that love exists?' Like this, you should loudly oppose each and every thing. Don't waste even a single opportunity that comes your way to dispute anything that people say. Criticize their views and ask for proof. They won't be able to prove anything. Then, they will become the fools and you, who question and criticize everything, will be deemed highly intelligent." The young man promised to obey the mahātmā.

Many years later, the mahātmā returned to the village. As soon as he arrived, the villagers went to him and exclaimed, "After your last visit, a miracle took place in this village. One fine morning, a fool suddenly became a wise man. He is now unbelievably smart and intelligent!"

The mahātmā understood who the villagers were talking about. The man came to see him and said, "Your advice was very effective. Now, as far as the villagers are concerned, I'm highly intelligent!"

The mahātmā laughed and said, "Don't tell anyone the secret!"

Amma is not saying that logic and intelligence are unnecessary or that they ought to be discarded. What Amma is trying to say is that we must disabuse ourselves of the view that they are everything. Use the intellect and logic where they are needed. But there are innumerable occasions in life when we must communicate with the heart of another person. On those occasions, we must use the language of love, patience and faith.

If we were asked, "What is the meaning of life?" we might give an answer based on our experiences. But our answer might not explain the real meaning of life. The intellect and logic are insufficient if we wish to experience the true meaning and scope of life. We must transcend intellect and logic and look upon life with eyes of love and faith. We must cultivate the attitude of welcoming everything with self-surrender. Then all situations and experiences will become as sweet as nectar. This is the path that spirituality shows us.

The Beauty of a Child

Children, childlike innocence has a special place in spirituality. All the spiritual masters in the world point to childlike innocence as an expression of the spiritual perfection lying dormant in us. A child has no thought of the past or the future. All of his attention is on what he is doing. So, we can say that the child lives only in the present moment.

Everything a child does has a special charm. That is why we always feel close to and affectionate towards all children. Even the stone-hearted will have a soft spot for children. Only the mentally deranged and those with demonic natures won't have such feelings for children.

A child is without an ego. If a child smiles at us, we will instinctively return the smile. If a child stretches its hand out with some food, we will not be able to refuse it even if the food is dirty. If we see a child crying, our mind will naturally melt. This is because a child's love is pure and untainted. What taints us is the ego. Everyone feels drawn to a child because it has no ego. The innocent heart of a child is a symbol of the spiritual purity that is latent in human beings. But a child's innocence is only temporary. When it grows, its mind will be tainted by the ego and other impurities. Yet, purity and innocence are buried within each person. Through spiritual practice and discipline, we can recover and sustain this purity and innocence.

If we closely observe young children, we can learn from them many good qualities that we ought to cultivate in life. Innocence is one such quality. Another is optimistic faith. Look at a toddler as it tries to stand and walk. It falls many times. It cries in pain. Sometimes, it might injure itself. Yet, it will get up and continue trying to walk. It will never give up. No child in the world thinks, "I've been trying to walk for so many days and have fallen down more than a hundred times. My body is hurting. I'm giving up. I don't want to walk. I'll spend the rest of my life crawling." It will continue trying to walk again and again, even if it falls down a thousand times and gets hurt in the process. This quality of a child—its tireless enthusiasm that is not dampened by failures or disappointments—is a great lesson that we ought to learn. It is the biggest example of unwavering faith and an indomitable will.

Likewise, children are always living in the here and now, whereas we are usually engrossed in thoughts of the past or worries of the future. One is gone and the other is yet to come. Neither are real. Reality lies in the present moment. But we forget to live in the present moment. All action takes place in the present. We feel love and happiness in the present moment. This does not mean that we don't need to plan anything. When an engineer is creating a blueprint for a bridge, he must be focused on that task. When he is building the bridge, he must focus on the construction. Instead, if he muses about the past or the future, both blueprint and bridge will be flawed.

A man went into an ice cream parlor and ordered his favorite chocolate ice cream. When he received the ice cream, he thought, "I don't know why, but since this morning, I've been having a headache. I've already taken three painkillers, but the pain is still persisting. Maybe, it's a symptom of some disease and I should see the doctor. Should I go for a scan? Maybe, some poison entered my system. I noticed that many of the food vessels in the restaurant where I dined last evening were not covered. Perhaps a lizard or cockroach fell into one of them. Maybe it was a spider!"

While thus musing, he noticed a fancy car stopping in front of the ice cream parlor. A man wearing expensive clothes, a gold watch and gold-framed spectacles got out. The man thought, "Only rich people can afford all that. Poor people like me can't even dream of such a lifestyle! O God, even if I don't get to buy such an expensive car or stylish clothes, please let me have a small car and fashionable clothes that look good on me." He sat there fantasizing about traveling in his own car, wearing expensive clothes, and strutting about in front of others.

Suddenly, he came back to his senses. "O God! Here I am, sitting in an ice cream parlor. Where is my ice cream?" He had already finished it but had not been able to relish even a spoonful. Many of us are like this. We waste our time on useless thoughts of the past or on being anxious about the future. The contentment and happiness of the present moment are lost on us.

Look at a child. It is always living in the present moment. It is not concerned about the next moment or about what went before. It does not have either past or future, only the present moment. This is the secret of the child's beauty, innocence and attraction.

We have not completely lost this innocence because it is our true nature. It will never cease to be because it exists in the depths of our mind. If a mirror is dusty, we cannot see our reflection clearly. Likewise, the mirror of our innocence has become dusty. We must wipe away the dust. That is the purpose of spiritual practices. When we meditate and do *japa* (repeated chanting of a mantra) regularly and resolutely, our thoughts will subside and the mind will become still. Then we will realize that this perfect innocence was always within us. We will become aware that it is our true nature.

The Benefits of Forgiving

Children, some people ask Amma, "Every religious text and spiritual teacher teaches that we must cultivate a mind that forgives the mistakes of others. But how to forgive those who perpetrate horrible crimes? How can we forgive those who commit atrocities against helpless women and children?"

Pointing a finger at wrongdoers and taking legal action against them isn't wrong at all. If we let criminals go unpunished, they might repeat the same crime. Not only that, if the criminal is allowed to go scot-free, others may become emboldened to do the same crime. Many innocent people will suffer as a result.

In the West, if criminals who are apprehended are found to be mentally unsound, they are not imprisoned like other criminals. Instead, they are housed in special facilities for treatment. If they are addicted to alcohol or drugs, they are rehabilitated so that they can become free of their addiction. One who has been convicted of molesting women will always remain under police surveillance. He will not be permitted access to places frequented by women and children. When medical treatment is combined with police supervision to treat criminals with mental illness, they rarely repeat the crime.

It is also important to restore the mental health of the victims of crimes. Naturally, they will be angry, distressed and vengeful. But such feelings will make them sick. This is why it is said that one must forgive. Victims must be counseled and trained to meditate and pray.

Amma is reminded of a story. A young woman's right hand became paralyzed. She went to a doctor but different treatments did not yield any result. Finally, she went to see a psychologist, who spoke to her for a while and asked if there had been any incident in the recent past that distressed her. The young woman replied, "My mother died when I was young. Then my father remarried. After they had children of their own, my stepmother took a dislike to me. She started scolding me for each and every thing. She found fault with everything I did. Last week, her taunts were more than I could bear. I couldn't control my anger and even felt like hitting her. Somehow, I controlled my anger but with great difficulty. Since then, I haven't spoken to her."

The psychologist told her, "You managed to control your anger outwardly, but it's still there, deep in your subconscious. The emotions we suppress affect our health adversely. That has happened to you. You hand became paralyzed because of the anger you're suppressing."

Convinced that this diagnosis was true, the young woman took steps to release her anger and hatred of her stepmother. Gradually, the condition of her hand normalized.

In a sense, the urge to commit a crime is a mental disease. When circumstances that incite this criminal inclination arise, criminals lose their ability to think rationally and so, they do wrong. Once we understand this, we will feel sorry for them and be able to forgive their mistakes.

Know Yourself. Know Others.

Children, there are good and bad qualities in everyone. Finding fault with others doesn't help anyone. It creates unnecessary tension and turbulence in our minds, and destroys our peace and happiness. We must try to see and accept the good in others. This is especially important in family life. Often, when we speak about our life partner to others, knowingly or unknowingly, we highlight their small flaws and foibles, even if only for fun. We might share these during gatherings with family or friends. If the partners love and trust each other, these critiques might not create any problem. But these days, even such small criticisms lead to huge rows in families.

We must always talk only about the strengths of the other person and never reveal their weaknesses in front of others. The shortcomings of husband and wife must never become a topic of conversation among others. They should remain a secret between the spouses. Instead of criticizing and finding fault with each other, they must try to solve their interpersonal problems. Otherwise, we might provoke an angry reaction from the other person. The spouse's faults must not be used as a weapon against him or her. Point out his or her mistakes if you have to, but do so lovingly. The intention behind our words must be to do good, to find solutions to the problems.

Women and men are like two different worlds. There is a huge gulf between the physical, emotional and intellectual worlds they inhabit. The relationship between spouses will become smooth only if both have considerable patience, forbearance, love and trust. Otherwise, there will always be conflict and confrontation between their two worlds. Even today, society expects women to forgive and forbear. It is true that women ought to have these qualities because a woman is also a mother, the first teacher of her child, and the one who guides her husband along the path of dharma. She must be a role model so that the family can be united, and the bond between husband and wife can be resilient. But it is wrong to think that only women need to be patient and forbearing and that men don't need to be. The qualities of motherhood are necessary for both man and woman.

Patience, forbearance, love and compassion are all womanly qualities. This is what Amma means by motherhood. Both men and women ought to be equally endowed with these qualities. Only then will harmony and rhythm prevail in family and social life. Only then will men and women be able to understand each other. Even though many men nod their heads in a show of agreement, they do not really try to understand women. They expect women to be submissive to them.

Many people ask, "How can we get rid of these flaws?" First of all, we must be able to identify our flaws and accept them. We must see how these flaws mar our individuality, that they are obstacles preventing us from fulfilling our potential and maximizing our abilities. Transformation takes place only when we realize the need to change. Once we realize and accept our flaws, we will sincerely want to change and correct our weaknesses. The most effective way to do that is to become aware of our shortcomings and to accept that we have them.

Amma is reminded of an incident that happened in a hospital in Mumbai. A devotee told Amma about it. Many people chew *pān* (tobacco and areca nut wrapped in betel leaves) in Mumbai. They tend to spit out the chewed pān wherever they are, without thinking twice about it. The walls of the hospital elevator were splattered with the red pān juice spat out by those who used the elevator. No matter how many times the walls were cleaned, it would become splattered with the red pān juice soon after. The hospital authorities pondered ways to solve this problem. Finally, they affixed large mirrors on the four walls of the elevator.

People stopped spitting the chewed pān. Why? They started seeing themselves in the mirror as they spat out the sticky red liquid. When they realized how grotesque their habit was, they stopped it.

Let us also try to become aware of our own shortcomings. Once we recognize them, we can relinquish them without being pushed by anyone. Only when we truly see our flaws will we understand how ugly and dishonorable they are. At present, we are not aware of the negative influence that these habits have on our personality, because our egoism and ignorance have clouded our inner clarity. Therefore, we are not able to overcome them. But when the light of awareness dawns, we will be able to see the distortions in our personality and get rid of them. Then we will find greater joy and contentment both within the family and in other spheres of life.

Glossary

abhiṣēka: ceremonial 'bathing' of an image of a deity by pouring water, milk and other liquids.

adharma: unrighteousness; deviation from natural harmony.

akṣara: imperishable; denotes Brahman, the Supreme; also means alphabet or letter.

Amma: 'mother' in Malayāḷam and various other Indian languages.

Arjuna: great archer and one of the heroes of the *Mahābhārata.* It is Arjuna whom Kṛṣṇa addresses in the *Bhagavad Gītā.*

āśrama: one of the four stages of life in traditional India; they include *brahmacarya* (celibate student life), *gārhasthya* (householder life), *vānaprastha* (retired life dedicated to spiritual practices) and *sannyāsa* (life of complete renunciation); also, a halting place or hermitage.

ātmā: Self or soul.

ātma-kṛpa: one's own grace.

avatār: from Sanskrit root *'ava-tarati'* — 'to come down.' Divine incarnation.

Bhāgavata Purāṇa: see *Śrīmad Bhāgavatam.*

bhakti: devotion for God.

Bhīma: second of the five Pāṇḍava brothers; character in the *Mahābhārata*; rival of Duryōdhana.

Buddha: from *'budh,'* meaning 'to wake up;' also, a reference to Sage Gautama Buddha, a spiritual master whose teachings form the foundation of Buddhism.

Dēvī: Goddess / Divine Mother.

Dēvī Bhāgavatam: also known as *Dēvī Bhāgavata Purāṇa*, it deals with the worship of Dēvī or Śakti, the mother of all beings and the bestower of spiritual liberation.

Dēvī Māhātmyam: also known as *Durgā Saptaśatī* and *Chaṇḍī*, it is part of the *Mārkaṇḍēya Purāṇa* (chapters 81 – 93); text glorifying Dēvī in the form of Durgā, the protector of devotees.

dharma: 'that which upholds (creation).' Generally refers to the harmony of the universe, a righteous code of conduct, sacred duty or eternal law.

dīpārādhana: ceremony in which the Divine is worshipped by waving a lighted camphor.

Durgā: consort of Lord Śiva; also called Umā and Pārvatī; Goddess known for defeating demons and protecting devotees; one of the forms of Dēvī worshipped during Navarātri.

Durvāsa: a legendary *ṛṣi* known for his flaming temper.

Duryōdhana: the eldest of the Kaurava brothers; antagonist of the Pāṇḍava brothers; an evil character in the *Mahābhārata*.

gṛhastha: householder; member of the second of four *āśramas* (stages of life), which include *brahmacarya* (celibate student life), *gṛhasthāśrama* (married householder life), *vānaprastha* (life of retirement and contemplation) and *sannyāsa*.

gṛhasthāśrama: see *gṛhastha*.

gṛhasthāśrami: one who follows the *gṛhasthāśrama* lifestyle.

guṇa: one of three types of qualities, *viz.* sattva, rajas and tamas. Human beings express a combination of these qualities. Sāttvic

qualities are associated with calmness and wisdom, rajas with activity and restlessness, and tamas with dullness or apathy.
Guru: spiritual teacher.

iṣṭa-dēvatā: preferred form of divinity.

Jagadambā: 'Mother of the Universe;' the Divine Mother.
japa: repeated chanting of a mantra.
jñāna: knowledge of the Truth. A ***jñānī*** is one who knows the Truth.

Kāḷakūṭa: the deadly poison that emerged during the churning of the Ocean of Milk and which Lord Śiva swallowed and retained in his throat, causing the blueness of his neck.
karma: action; mental, verbal and physical activity; chain of effects produced by our actions.
Karṇa: the first son of Kuntī and thus the brother of the Pāṇḍavas. However, as he was born before Kuntī's marriage, she gave him away, and Karṇa was adopted by a charioteer. Later, he befriended Duryōdhana and fought on the side of the Kauravas against the Pāṇḍavas during the Mahābhārata War.
Kauravas: the 101 children of King Dhṛtarāṣṭra and Queen Gāndhārī, of whom the unrighteous Duryōdhana was the eldest. The Kauravas were the enemies of their cousins, the virtuous Pāṇḍavas, whom they fought against in the Mahābhārata War.
Kṛṣṇa: from '*kṛṣ*,' meaning 'to draw to oneself' or 'to remove sin;' principal incarnation of Lord Viṣṇu. He was born into a royal family but raised by foster parents, and lived as a cowherd boy in Vṛndāvan, where he was loved and worshipped by his devoted companions, the *gōpīs* (milkmaids) and *gōpas* (cowherd boys). Kṛṣṇa later established the city of Dwāraka. He was a friend and advisor to his cousins, the Pāṇḍavas, especially Arjuna, whom

he served as charioteer during the Mahābhārata War, and to whom he revealed his teachings as the *Bhagavad Gītā.*

kuṇḍalinī śakti: Spiritual power, personified as a snake coiled in the muladhara cakra, a psychic center of spiritual power located near the coccyx, at the base of the spine. During the process of spiritual awakening, the snake of spiritual power rises through the spinal column and ultimately reaches the sahasrara, or crown cakra, envisaged as a thousand-petal lotus; this is when one attains spiritual enlightenment.

Kuntī: mother of Karṇa and the five Pāṇḍava brothers; character in the *Mahābhārata.*

Lakṣmī: consort of Lord Viṣṇu; Goddess of Fortune; a form of Dēvī, the Goddess; one of the forms of Dēvī worshipped during Navarātri.

Lalitā Sahasranāma: 1,000 names of Śrī Lalitā Dēvī, a form of the Goddess.

Mahābali: an ancient king, whose rule was characterized by auspiciousness and abundance; owing to pride in his generosity, Lord Viṣṇu appeared before him in the guise of Vāmana, who asked Mahābali for three paces of land. Mahābali acceded to the request. Vāmana grew in size and covered the three worlds in two steps. With nothing else to offer him other than his ego, Mahābali bowed down in an attitude of surrender to the Lord. Mahābali is associated with Ōṇam.

Mahābhārata: ancient Indian epic that Sage Vyāsa composed, depicting the war between the righteous Pāṇḍavas and the unrighteous Kauravas.

mahātmā: 'great soul;' term used to describe one who has attained spiritual realization.

Malayāḷam: language spoken in the Indian state of Kerala.
mantra: a sound, syllable, word or words of spiritual content. According to Vēdic commentators, mantras are revelations of ṛṣis arising from deep contemplation.
Māyā: cosmic delusion, personified as a temptress. Illusion; appearance, as contrasted with reality; the creative power of the Lord.
mōkṣa: spiritual liberation, i.e. release from the cycle of births and deaths.
mūlādhāra: one of the seven *cakras* or centers of psychic power located near the coccyx, at the base of the spine.

Navarātri: literally 'nine nights,' Navarātri is a Hindu festival celebrated in the month of *Aświni* (September – October). It is dedicated to the worship of the Divine Mother, primarily in the forms of Durgā, Lakṣmī and Saraswatī.

Ōṇam: Kerala's biggest festival, occurring in the month of *Ciṅṅam* (August – September).

Pāṇḍavas: five sons of King Pāṇḍu, and cousins of Kṛṣṇa.
Pārvatī: consort of Lord Śiva.
pāyasam: sweet pudding.
prāṇa: breath; vital force.
prasād: blessed offering or gift from a holy person or temple, often in the form of food.
Purāṇas: compendium of stories, including the biographies and stories of gods, saints, kings and great people; allegories and chronicles of great historical events that aim to make the teachings of the Vēdas simple and available to all.

rajas: see *guṇa.*

Rāma: divine hero of the *Rāmāyaṇa*. An incarnation of Lord Viṣṇu, Rāma is considered the ideal man of *dharma* and virtue. '*Ram*' means 'to revel;' one who revels in himself; the principle of joy within; one who gladdens the hearts of others.
Rāmāyaṇa: 24,000-verse epic poem on the life and times of Rāma.
Rāvaṇa: powerful demon king. Viṣṇu incarnated as Lord Rāma to kill him and thereby restore harmony to the world.
ṛṣi: spiritually enlightened being and seer to whom mantras and the secrets of the universe were revealed in deep meditation.

sādhana: regimen of disciplined and dedicated spiritual practice that leads to the supreme goal of Self-realization.
sahaja samādhi: the highest state of spiritual enlightenment in which pure and silent non-dual awareness coexists with an ability to continue using the human faculties.
samādhi: literally, 'cessation of all mental movements;' oneness with God; a transcendental state in which one loses all sense of individual identity; union with absolute reality; a state of intense concentration in which consciousness is completely unified.
sahasrāra: the 'thousand-petalled' crown cakra; the seventh and highest cakra or psychic center in the body; when the spiritual practitioner raises his *kuṇḍalinī śakti* to this cakra, he or she attains spiritual enlightenment.
samskāra: a personality trait conditioned over many lives or one life: a mental and behavioural pattern; a latency or tendency within the mind which will manifest itself if given the proper environment or stimulus.
Sanātana Dharma: literally, 'Eternal Religion' or 'Eternal Way of Life,' the original and traditional name of Hinduism.
sannyāsī: monk who has taken formal vows of renunciation (*sannyāsa*); traditionally wears an ocher-colored robe,

representing the burning away of all desires. The female equivalent is ***sannyāsinī.***

Saraswatī: Goddess of Learning and the Arts; consort of Lord Brahma, the Creator; one of the forms of the Divine Mother worshipped during Navarātri.

***sat-cit-ānanda*:** truth-consciousness-bliss; a term that is used to suggest the nature of the indescribable Brahman (Supreme).

satsaṅg: communion with the Supreme Truth. Also, being in the company of *mahātmās*, studying the scriptures, and listening to the enlightening talks of a mahātmā; a meeting of people to listen to and/or discuss spiritual matters; a spiritual discourse.

sattva: see *guṇa.*

sēvā: selfless service, the results of which are dedicated to God.

***Śakti*:** principle of feminine energy; primordial power.

Śiva: worshipped as the first and the foremost in the lineage of Gurus, and as the formless substratum of the universe in relationship to Śakti. The Lord of Destruction in the Hindu Trinity.

***Śiva-liṅga*:** literally, 'emblem of Śiva.' An abstract representation of the beginningless and endless nature of the Divine.

Śivarātri: literally, 'night of Śiva,' a festival dedicated to worshipping Lord Śiva and celebrated in the month of *Phālguna* or *Māgha* (February – March): Devotees observe this festival by fasting and keeping a night-long vigil doing spiritual practices.

***Śrīmad Bhāgavatam*:** also known as *Bhāgavatam* or *Bhāgavata Purāṇa*, a Sanskrit composition that upholds devotion to Lord Viṣṇu, the Sustainer in the Hindu Trinity. It is one of the 18 Purāṇas. It narrates the life, pastimes and teachings of various incarnations of Viṣṇu, chiefly that of Lord Kṛṣṇa.

tamas: see *guṇa.*

tapas: austerities, penance; a *tapasvī* is one who engages in tapas.
tattwattile bhakti: devotion rooted in knowledge of the difference between the eternal and the ephemeral.

Upavāsam: literally 'to live near' (God); figuratively used to refer to fasting.

Vāli: character in the *Rāmāyaṇa*; ruler of Kiṣkindhā and brother of Sugrīva; owing to a conflict between him and his brother, Vāli banished Sugrīva from the kingdom and married Ruma, Sugrīva's wife. Sugrīva sought the help of Lord Rāma, who killed Vāli.
Vāmana: an incarnation of Lord Viṣṇu. He took the form of a young Brāhmin boy who asked Mahābali for three paces of land. When Mahābali acceded to this request, Vāmana grew in size and covered all the worlds in two steps. He placed his third step on Mahābali's head, a gesture symbolizing the Lord's conquest of the devotee's ego.
Vidyārambham: a ceremony in which a young child is initiated into learning.
Vijayadaśamī: the 10th day (*daśamī*), or day after, Navarātri. It denotes the victory (*vijaya*) of good over evil.
Viṣṇu: Lord of Sustenance in the Hindu Trinity.
Viṣu: popular Hindu festival celebrated in Kerala and which coincides with the spring equinox.
Viṣukkaṇi: 'that which is first seen on Viṣu.' It refers to the arrangement of items that are considered auspicious, and which are placed at the altar. Traditionally, the elders in the family light the lamp at the altar on the morning of Viṣu. The others in the family are led there with their eyes closed. When the open their eyes, the first thing they behold is the Viṣukkaṇi.

Vṛndāvan: pilgrimage destination in present-day Uttar Pradesh, India, associated with the childhood days and youth of Lord Kṛṣṇa.

Pronunciation Guide

Vowels can be short or long:
a – as 'u' in but; ā – as 'a' in far
e – as 'a' in may; ē – as 'a' in name
i – as 'i' in pin; ī – as 'ee' in meet
o – as in oh; ō – as 'o' in mole
u – as 'u' in push; ū – as 'oo' in hoot

ṛ – as ri in crisp
ḥ – pronounce 'aḥ' like 'aha,' 'iḥ' like 'ihi,' and 'uḥ' like 'uhu.'

Some consonants are aspirated (e.g. kh); others are not (e.g. k). The examples given below are only approximate:
k – as 'k' in 'kite;' kh – as 'ckh' in 'Eckhart'
g – as 'g' in 'give;' gh – as 'g-h' in 'dig-hard'
c – as 'c' in 'cello;' ch – as 'ch-h' in 'staunch-heart'
j – as 'j' in 'joy;' jh – as 'dgeh' in 'hedgehog'
p – as 'p' in 'pine;' ph – as 'ph' in 'up-hill'
b – as 'b' in 'bird;' bh – as 'bh' in 'rub-hard'

r – as 'r' in ride
ñ – as 'ny' in 'canyon;' ṅ – as 'ng' in 'sing'

The letters ḍ, ṭ, ṇ are pronounced with the tip of the tongue against the hard palate, the others with the tip against the teeth.
ṭ – as 't' in 'tub;' ṭh – as 'th' in 'lighthouse'
ḍ – as 'd' in 'dove;' ḍh – as 'dh' in 'red-hot'
ṇ – as 'n' in 'naught'
ḷ – as 'l' in 'revelry'
ṣ – as 'sh' in 'shine;' ś – as 's' in German 'sprechen'

With double consonants the sound is pronounced twice:
cc – as 'tc' in 'hot chip'
jj – as 'dj' in 'red jet'

www.ingramcontent.com/pod-product-compliance
Lightning Source LLC
Chambersburg PA
CBHW071210090426
42736CB00014B/2764
* 9 7 8 1 6 8 0 3 7 8 9 8 6 *